Industrialization
Economic Development
and the Regional Question
in the Third World

Studies in Society and Space

Series editors **A J Scott** and **M Storper**

p Pion Limited, 207 Brondesbury Park, London NW2 5JN

Industrialization Economic Development and the Regional Question in the Third World

from Import Substitution to Flexible Production

M Storper

p Pion Limited, 207 Brondesbury Park, London NW2 5JN

British Library Cataloguing in Publication Data
A CIP catalogue record for this book is available from the British Library.

ISBN 0 85086 149 7

Printed in Great Britain by Page Bros (Norwich) Limited

Acknowledgements

This book was written with the support of an American Republics Research Grant from the US Fulbright Commission in 1986.

I wish to thank not only the Fulbright Commission, but the Faculty of Economics and Administration at the University of São Paulo, and especially Professor Carlos R Azzoni, for support during the preparation of this work.

I also benefited from comments made by participants at seminars where various parts of this analysis were presented. These included: the Federal University of Pará, Belém; Federal University of Ceará, Fortaleza; Federal University of Santa Catarina, Florianópolis; Catholic University of Rio de Janeiro; Federal University of Rio de Janeiro; Federal University of Minas Gerais; The University of São Paulo, Rio Claro; and the University of São Paulo. I received many helpful suggestions and insights from Brazilian colleagues who are too numerous to name here.

I would especially like to thank Professor Armen Mamigonian of the Federal University of Santa Catarina for guiding me through the industries of that state, and Professor Campolina Diniz of CEDEPLAR in Belo Horizonte for his hospitality.

I would also like to acknowledge the personal support of Marilia Andrade and Carlos Alberto Doria during my stay in Brazil.

Supplemental funds came from the Academic Senate and the Institute of Industrial Relations at the University of California, Los Angeles. Very able research assistance was provided by Carlos Quandt and Mei-Po Kwan, and secretarial help by the staff of the Graduate School of Urban Planning at UCLA, especially Tony Miranda. I am grateful to all for their assistance.

Contents

Contents

Introduction

The theme of this book is the relationship of spatial polarization of economic activity and of population to national economic development in the countries currently classified as 'semi-industrialized', such as Brazil, Korea, and Mexico. This analysis is concerned with the role of spatial polarization in the transition from primarily agricultural economies into industrial economies, and the relationship between the condition of geographical polarization and the subsequent path of industrialization, urbanization, and national development.

The main reason for evaluating the role of polarization is that it is politically and economically important. Planning authorities in many countries, as well as international development agencies, have been preoccupied in recent years with the problems of the great industrial regions at the centers of these economies. São Paulo, Mexico City, and Seoul are said to represent a phenomenon labelled 'overurbanization'. Planners want to reduce pollution, traffic, and social marginality found in the great urban centers of the Third World by installing in these places systems of territorial management. At the same time, there is great concern with the underdevelopment and poverty in the peripheral regions of these countries' national territories, places such as the Northeast and Amazonian regions of Brazil, and the northern and southern extremes of Mexico.

Much analysis of regional development in developing countries holds that some of the developmental failures of peripheral regions are precisely a result of the higher level of development found in the great industrial poles; the center is frequently said to thrive on 'urban bias' in development policy, and thus the underdevelopment of the periphery is seen as a consequence of the center's own growth (Lipton, 1977). Indeed, much of the history of explicit regional policies in a country such as Brazil has followed from precisely this type of assumption. In one form or another, much of this regional policy is founded on the idea of redistribution of industrial activity away from the great industrial regions toward the regional peripheries of the national economy. It is assumed that redistribution can attenuate interregional inequalities and resolve simultaneously the problems both of the centers and of the peripheries. Various methods have been proposed to achieve this goal, ranging from industrial – urban growth poles in peripheral regions to support for 'bottom- up' local economic development in peripheral areas. Regional planning agencies and scholars from a variety of fields have been deeply involved in advancing the rationales for these regional development programs for several decades.

Yet it is rare that the underlying assumptions of these policies and programs are analyzed. For example, it is commonly assumed, in the literature, that regionally uneven development is bad, in and of itself, and that therefore reducing it by whatever means will be good for a society (Gore, 1984). The premise of this book is that this idea cannot be defended simply on normative grounds. It must be justified via specific arguments about the role of polarization or regionally uneven development in the economic and social development process as a whole. That is, it must be demonstrated how polarization affects the outcomes of development processes generally before decisions can be made about regional policies. In this book I advance a theoretical framework for explaining the relationship between the spatial polarization of industrial activity and the processes of industrialization and national economic development in the semi-industrialized countries of the Third World, and use as my principal illustration the case of Brazil.

I then place this framework in the context of contemporary changes in the world economy and its dominant industrial systems and reevaluate the basis for industrial and regional policy. The book treats the main forms of industrial-regional policy that have been used in Latin America in recent years—especially that of import substitution. It then takes up the transition from a capitalism based on Fordist mass production to one based increasingly on production flexibility and traces the implications of this transition for Third World industrialization and policy choices. I attempt to demonstrate that there is little distinction between a valid industrial policy and a potentially successful regional economic development policy—both are concerned with the same processes.

1

The theoretical background

1.1 Theories of polarized development

Concern with the relationship between polarization and the process of industrialization and economic development in the Third World dates from the early and seminal contributions of Hirschman (1958) and Myrdal (1957), who in turn drew from the initial approaches to the subject made by Hoselitz (1953; 1955). Polarization refers to the condition in which a very large share of a country's economic activity (especially industry) or population is concentrated in one or a small number of cities or regions. 'Polarization reversal', a relatively recent concept, refers to a point at which a country begins, definitively, to distribute a greater proportion of its economic activity or population outside of its central region and into other regions of the national territory (Richardson, 1980). In this book, we are concerned with regional *polarization* and *interregional* polarization reversal. Polarization and depolarization (or concentration and dispersion) of population and economic activity are treated both as *states* of an economy and as *moments in a process* of economic development. The debate over polarization centers on defining the process. For example, does the process of industrialization of a nation commence with geographical polarization of industrial activity and end with its dispersal and thus the elimination of regional inequalities? If so, what makes such a process unfold?

Two basic responses to this question have been articulated. The first, or 'modernization' perspective, holds that polarization is essential to the initiation of modern development, but that regional inequalities produced by polarization are eventually reduced as development proceeds, through a process of naturally occurring polarization reversal. The second position holds that polarization is either unnecessary to development, or that it actually may retard the development potential of peripheral regions and distort the development path of the national economy itself. Let us take up the former first. The modernization perspective is based on elegantly articulated propositions about macroeconomic development which are underpinned by microeconomic models. To begin with the macroeconomic side, Alonso (1980) sums up much of the modernization perspective in his notion of "five bell shapes in development": (1) development stages, (2) income inequality, (3) regional inequality, (4) geographic concentration, and (5) demographic transition. The idea is that all these curves have a bell shape, rising at first, reaching an inflection point, and then falling as the economy matures. The main precondition for inflection is the strong interaction between development of the forces of production [a notion derived from Rostow (1961)] and eventual reduction in income inequality (the 'Kuznets effect') that propels the economy forward. The theory is basically neoclassical, with increased output and savings propelling investment, and tightening labor markets generating higher incomes. As a consequence, other supply-side changes come into play: with higher incomes, a demographic transition is effected in the form of reduced fertility levels (curve 5) and the geographic concentration of population (curve 4) slows because of economy-wide income increases which tend to be spatially equalizing owing to the simultaneous movement of economic activity (curve 3) to offset increases in factor prices (wages) in polarized industrial regions. The prime motors of all these changes are thus capital accumulation (investment) and changes in relative factor prices and quantities, generally and spatially. It should be noted that the second halves of these curves (that is, after the inflection point) have never been definitively observed in the developing countries. Only recently did Richardson (1980) advance the intriguing notion that Brazil had entered the stage of polarization reversal, but much dispute remains over whether his observation is empirically valid (Azzoni, 1986).

The microeconomic perspective is also that of the urban and regional scale. Polarization is attributed to the existence of external economies of scale. Up to a certain point, as the size of a city increases, its economic efficiency or productivity increases. In the initial stages of industrialization, a country experiences rural–urban migration; urbanization permits scale economies which are necessary to conserve scarce resources in the initial stages of industrialization. There exists a long and often torturous debate over what the 'optimal' (that is, productivity-maximizing) size of an urban agglomeration is, and whether large Third World industrial centers have passed this limit (Hansen, 1978; Henderson, 1982; Mera, 1973; Richardson, 1973; Wheaton and Shishido, 1981).

Linked to these ideas about individual cities is the idea of an optimal or normal type of urban system as the culmination of the process of economic development. We should note at the outset that virtually all research on urban hierarchies is carried out in terms of population, rather than economic activity, yet the underlying concept is that there exist normal geographical distributions of both these factors. The normal relationship is, of course, the rank-size rule. That is, as the number of cities of a given size increases the size of the cities decreases, whereas as the size of cities increases, the number of units in the size class drops, a relationship which has been observed in many countries. The strict version of the rank-size rule holds that in an optimal urban hierarchy, the cities in each size class are precise multiples of the sizes of cities in the size class below them (see Zipf, 1949). This rule has not been confirmed, however, because different national systems of cities exhibit different quantitative relationships between rank-orders (see Storper and Walker, 1989, chapter 1), with some countries having a large role for middle-size cities (for example, West Germany), others having a very large capital city relative to the country's population (France, Great Britain) and others coming closer to the strict rank-size distribution (the USA, Canada).

Polarization represents a dramatic, but rather a common, case of deviation from the strict rank-size rule, where one or a few cities in the nation's urban system are responsible for a very large proportion of the nation's population or economic activity (or both), a phenomenon known as 'urban primacy'. The polar cities or regions are then called 'primate' areas. In Brazil, for example, the São Paulo metropolis is primate in terms of industrial activity, but not in terms of population (31% of the nation's industry; 12% of its population) (Azzoni, 1986). The state of São Paulo, which cannot be judged by the concept of primacy, nonetheless concentrates 51.3% of the nation's industry. Buenos Aires, on the other hand, is dramatically primate in both respects, as is Mexico City.

It should be noted that policy is not exclusively concerned with primate cities and regions; it is, more broadly, preoccupied with *very big* cities and regions, and conversely with the fates of regions which do not receive very much investment in the course of national industrialization and lag progressively further behind the big cities and regions. Indeed, in the end a precise theoretical or empirical definition of primacy seems less important than the substantive issue of whether laggard regions will ultimately enter into a dynamic development process, as well as the nature of the relationship between the growth of big cities and the process of economic development.

The modernization perspective described above leads easily to broad conclusions about the relationship between urbanization and national development. In a number of comparative city-system studies it has been argued that the differences observed between countries—that is, the deviations from the rank-size rule—are largely attributable to the level of economic development of each country. That is, less developed countries systematically show steeper urban hierarchies and greater urban and regional primacy, whereas more developed countries show the opposite (El Shaks, 1972). It follows, naturally, that development brings a more even urban hierarchy. The theoretical reasoning goes back to the five bell curves, and need not be repeated, except to note that the process of development being referred to is supposed to produce both consumption and production specialization so that the rank-size conception of the urban hierarchy conforms with that of central place theory. The city system consists of a hierarchy of units, each operating at different but efficient scales, according to its mix of activities.[1]

In all of this literature—the five bell shapes, urban size, and urban-regional hierarchies—the core notion is that concentration is initially efficient, that growth ultimately reduces productivity for the economy

[1] Actually, there is considerable dispute over whether the observations are historically valid, that is, whether urban hierarchies really do tend to even out with the level of economic development. In Europe, for example, many city systems are primate, in spite of a high level of development. The tendency to depolarization is observed much more frequently in terms of industrial activity than in terms of population or tertiary activity (Langenbruch, 1981).

as a whole through diseconomies of agglomeration, and therefore that polarization will be reduced in the process of development. In Myrdal's terms, 'spread' should overcome 'backwash', producing a new city-size distribution and reducing interregional inequalities. It is crucial at this point to emphasize the nature of explanation in these theories. In the five bell shapes, the emphasis is on macroeconomic price shifts, their spatial manifestations, and their effects on the spatial preferences both of capitalists (businesses) and of workers (residences).[2]

In these discussions, industry receives some analytical attention as a force behind initial polarization; as, for example, in Hirschman's discussion of the initiation of industrialization through the introduction of selective 'imbalances' in an industrial system. These imbalances are then resolved through the establishment of backward and forward linkages, resulting in localized industrial growth poles. This is also a theme which has been read into the work of Perroux (1955). But, when it comes to the reversal of polarization, the literature has little specifically to say about industrial development, or the locational behavior of economic activities, and, as a result, the theories of polarization and polarization reversal remain quite vague as to the actual mechanisms by which these processes are generated.

Finally, we should note the opposition position on the question of polarization.[3] Arrayed squarely against the modernization theories of regional development is a literature from the 1970s, in which it is argued that: polarization reflects a distorted type of capitalist development;

---

[2] In the literature on optimal urban size, the emphasis is on the costs of urban services and general effects of spatial packing in the course of development. In the city system literature, in general, there is no explanation other than reference to a generalized notion of 'development', except the Löschian central place theory, in which market sizes and market specializations are the central variables. There is a great deal of dispute over exactly how external economies, once formed, are broken down and a city system could begin to develop. Myrdal (1957) concluded that polarization was necessary for development, but he was also very pessimistic about the possibility for spread to overcome backwash. He argued that backwash would be continually renewed by local Keynesian income effects, which would continue to augment the scale of the existing centers at a greater rate than increases in the scale of peripheral places. Hirschman (1958) also saw the need for polarization, and felt that 'trickle-down' effects might be very small in peripheral regions. He therefore advocated encouraging the process of interregional growth transmission by trying to replicate the conditions for national development within particular subnational regions through growth pole strategies. Friedmann (1966; 1973), on the other hand, was more optimistic than Hirschman or Myrdal, arguing that national territorial integration, Rostovian growth of the forces of production, and adherence to the Kuznets law would ultimately reduce external economies in the center, while regional policies (especially territorial integration) could hasten the process and push development into smaller and more dispersed city units.

[3] These arguments will be considered in greater detail in chapter 6, and therefore receive only a brief treatment here.

it tends to depress the developmental impulses of peripheral regions; and by driving up factor prices it ultimately limits the process of national development as a whole. Polarized development is distorted because it relies on large-scale capital-intensive technologies which do not absorb labor and which require income concentration to support the consumption of industrial durable goods. It depresses the developmental impulses of peripheral regions by diverting potential investment capital away from them and by inducing rural–urban migration and thus depleting regions of their best human resources. It puts fetters on the process of development as a whole because these investments could propel more activity and output in peripheral regions (in particular in rural activities) than they do in capital-intensive urban industry, absorbing more labor and distributing income more equally. 'Urban bias', and not technical efficiency, is the source of polarization and such bias should therefore be eliminated (Lipton, 1977).

A Marxist perspective on interregional (or, for that matter, international) relations holds that rich regions exploit poor regions via 'unequal exchange' (Amin, 1974; Emmanuel, 1972). Here, poor regions engage in labor-intensive activities whereas rich regions engage in capital-intensive activities. Labor time is the source of value, but not of prices; as a result, the price system rewards rich regions in excess of their value creation, because their goods trade at high prices, and it discriminates against poor regions. The result is that the system of exchange prevents poor regions from accumulating capital and raising wages and, therefore, from developing in a way that would reduce interregional inequality.

1.2 How to reconsider polarization

The theories of polarization and regional development cited above are riddled with analytical and empirical problems. At the very least, cities and regions that are primate in terms of population should be treated separately from those that are primate in industrial and economic terms. Yet the modernization theorists frequently use aggregated evidence on populations as indicators of economies of scale and thus economic efficiency *in production*. This simply reverses the logical order of theorizing about industrial–economic primacy; in areas such as São Paulo, which is primate in terms of production but simply very large in terms of population, population growth has temporally and spatially followed the growth path of industrialization, not the other way around (Cano, 1981). In regions which are primate in terms of both population and economic activity, population polarization can only be understood in light of economic forces which push people out of rural areas and pull them into urban labor markets. This process shall be analyzed in detail in the chapters that follow.

Industry is the best place to look, among different kinds of economic activities, for the polarization of labor demand. By industry I mean, in general, manufacturing and certain parts of the tertiary, or service, sector.

These intermediate services (such as commercial banks and producer services) are not necessarily oriented toward final demand. They are better thought of as services provided to industries or industrially organized service complexes and so can be included under the rubric of 'industry' in general (compare Gershuny, 1982; Noyelle and Stanback, 1983; Walker, 1985).[4] The basic reason for focusing on these sectors is that in the contemporary world their locations are principally determined by the internal logic of their own development rather than by the presence of discrete and exogenous 'locational factors'. The extreme contrast is agriculture, which is heavily dependent on natural resources and climate and is by definition spatially extensive. Manufacturing and services provided to enterprises, on the other hand, enjoy significant internal and external economies of scale, which permit them to serve large market areas from a small number of geographical points. By virtue of this, they have only a weak locational tie to markets. Much of the output of these sectors is intermediate and thus by definition oriented toward a market of other producers and not toward population (final markets). Historically, major industry-serving infrastructures have been created in concert with the growth of great industrial core zones; they are not implanted before such development, with industry then following after. Thus, of all the sectors of the economy, it is industry that has the greatest possibilities, in principle, of polarizing or depolarizing the territorial economic system as a whole. Industrial location analysis is therefore the logical starting point for theorizing polarization, and industrialization is the developmental process most deserving of our attention.

In focusing on industry, we return to the basic orientation of Myrdal (1957) and Hirschman (1958) and, to a lesser degree, Friedmann (1966; 1973). All considered urban economic efficiency to be largely an outcome of the behavior of industrial systems, and economic growth a result of the internal dynamics of the process of industrialization. Rather than regarding development as somehow emerging out of shifts in quantities of the factors of production and their prices, all these authors considered it necessary to understand the way that development was embedded in concrete forces of production and the social and institutional relations

---

[4] Note that many of the European 'primate cities', including places such as Paris and London, are not simply primate because they dominate their country's industrial production, but because they command a large share of the nation's industrial tertiary sector, such as financial services. These services are not spatially oriented to final demand—they are agglomerated service-production complexes linked either to export markets in other regions of the nation or to foreign markets. Thus, these are not simply residues of precapitalist growth. Even though these cities continue to enjoy a strong government presence, they are also important contemporary production centers, if we include in production the tertiary part of the economy. Even Rio de Janeiro can properly be thought of as supported by the growth of industrial–tertiary activities, whose product it exports to other places.

attached to them. These authors all investigated how development was embodied in concrete industrial complexes, and how growth poles can be encouraged to form in poor regions in order to break the core–periphery relation.

Even in their work, however, the understanding of industrial location behavior in the course of industrialization and its relationship to economic growth generally remains unnecessarily aggregated and generalized. This book is intended to unravel some of the connections, to make the relations between the inner workings of production systems, location, urbanization, and national development more explicit by drawing together growth theory with location theory. Fortunately, there exists a body of dynamic growth theory which is explicitly rooted in the concrete organization of industrial systems. This line of thought stretches, in its modern version, from the work of Marshall and Allyn Young, through the likes of Keynes, Verdoorn, and Kaldor, among others, and involves insights that might be called, variously, neo-Smithian, neo-Marxian, or post-Keynesian. Young (1928) argued forcefully that the progressive development of the division of labor in the economy as a whole is the central endogenous source of economic growth in a capitalist economy, because it creates increasing external economies of scale. We shall see that the division of labor underlies a set of definite physical and organizational correlates of the industrial growth process; it can easily be demonstrated that there are then identifiable geographical tendencies in the rise and growth of modern industrial production systems. We can pinpoint the dynamic interactions of growth, location, and regional development such that the growth dynamics of an economy can be seen as inextricably intertwined with their regional or locational forms.

To begin with, I identify the foundations of location behavior in the development of the division of labor in industry. The division of labor is the primary source of external economies of scale, with which are associated particular types of spatial linkages. These external economies are responsible for the *endogenous* creation of regional factor markets in the course of industrialization. By understanding some of the microeconomic aspects of these processes of spatial resource creation, we can establish a firmer basis for agglomeration theory, and disaggregate and specify the particular *organizational* mechanisms that generate polarization, urbanization, and city-system development in an industrializing economy (chapter 2). Polarization is related to specific organizational characteristics of industry which are in turn related to specific characteristics of the growth process as a whole.

Next, I identify the concrete locational processes capable of leading to interregional depolarization of industrial activity, or polarization reversal in a developing country. These processes are the creation of new industrial complexes, new spatial growth centers, and new regional growth peripheries. Besides these specific organizational characteristics, I show that these processes are—first and foremost—the result of growth, but this growth in turn is only secondarily a response to changes in relative spatial factor prices (chapter 3).

The last observation has profound implications for any analysis of the prospects for polarization reversal or regional policy. As noted, much of the debate about polarization is based on comparisons of the spatial histories of developed countries to those of developing areas, observing that there is a strong and positive correlation between income and output levels and the spatial dispersion of development. Putting aside the question of whether these comparisons are empirically and historically accurate, is it the case that industrialization necessarily produces this type of growth and income increase? The record of virtually all Latin American economies is one in which many medium-term and long-term growth and development indicators are not tracking the histories of the rich countries. They are not even following the path of the industrialization process in the locality (compare Bacha, 1978; Sunkel, 1985). As a result, there are only very weak tendencies toward interregional polarization reversal, even in economies that continue to be industrially very dynamic, such as Brazil (chapter 4). In chapter 5, I lay out some of these constraints on macroeconomic growth and polarization reversal in Third World economies. Moreover, I show that some of the constraints have strong roots precisely in the regional form that development has taken. This then permits a response to the question raised in much of the literature on polarization, that is, whether polarization is *responsible* for inhibiting the development of other regions in the national territory (chapter 6).

I conclude the book by suggesting that any successful long-term regional economic policy must have both different goals and different means from many existing policies (chapters 7 and 8).

Industrialization, polarization, and the division of labor

Urbanization comes about for many reasons, including political and administrative ones, (Brasília, Washington; and formerly, Rio de Janeiro); the concentration of the consumption power of the middle and upper classes, old aristocracies, and bureaucrats (formerly Paris); concentration of administrative activities of state or private industries (Rio de Janeiro, New York, Paris today); the expulsion of people from rural areas (London in the 17th and 18th centuries; Bélem, Fortaleza, Recife, etc., today). None of these factors, however, is responsible for the concentration of modern economic activities in a limited number of dynamic industrial cities or growth regions. Industrial growth often accompanies population concentration, as is the case in contemporary Mexico City, but it does not necessarily do so, as the cities of the Brazilian Northeast so clearly demonstrate. It is to the tendency for strong regional concentration of economic activity in industrializing countries—as in the cases of Mexico City and the São Paulo region—that I address my analysis.

The basic model unfolds in three parts. First, I develop an explanation of agglomeration and industrialization (section 2.1). Second, I explain why city hierarchies develop in the course of industrialization (section 2.2). Third, I explore the bases of my location theory in classical economic thought and begin to draw out its linkages to the theory of economic growth generally and to urban and regional economics in particular (section 2.3).

2.1 Urbanization, agglomeration, and the division of labor [5]

Agglomeration economies develop endogenously in the course of industrialization. To understand this, we can begin with the fundamental proposition of Adam Smith—that the division of labor is limited by the extent of the market—perhaps the most famous expression in economic thought.

A new product begins to take form in various different workshops, probably simultaneously in different locations, as was the case with the early automobile industry, and more recently, with the electronics industry. As the product comes to be accepted and its market begins to grow, the division of labor—that is, specialization of functions within the production process—tends to deepen. This deepening of the *technical* division of labor may be accompanied by expansion of the *social* division of labor (the division of labor between different firms, each specializing in the production of intermediate inputs).

[5] This section owes much to the work of Allen Scott, and to work I have carried out jointly with him and with Susan Christopherson (see Scott, 1988a; 1988b; Scott and Storper, 1987; Storper and Christopherson, 1987; Storper and Scott, 1989a, 1989b).

With the further extension of the market, the potential to realize scale economies in production also grows. 'Economies of scale' describes in general the condition where increases in the quantity of output are an increasing function of growth in the quantities of inputs used in production. However, economies of scale may be realized either within a small number of firms or production units (internal economies of scale), or in the form of a complex of firms linked by market and quasi-market transactions. The latter type of scale economies are external economies (Young, 1928; see Storper, 1989). In the first case, the organization of production is relatively vertically and horizontally integrated. In the second case, the production process is more vertically and horizontally disintegrated.[6] Vertical integration occurs when the technical division of labor is managed by one firm or a restricted number of firms, or, in other words, when production is internalized under a firm's managerial hierarchy. This condition reflects the existence of 'economies of scope', or where the number of phases of the production process as a whole that can be efficiently integrated within the firm or unit of production is very large (Coase, 1937; Scott, 1988a; 1988b). In this case, the integrated enterprise has a large scope of activities, or labor processes, under its managerial control, and presumably this is because total production costs with integration are less than they would be were the process disintegrated. Where such economies of scope are minor or negative, however, then the different phases of the production process may be distributed among different specialized firms or production units, deepening the social division of labor.

There are many reasons for vertical disintegration, that is, many circumstances in which economies of scope are minor or negative. First, if the different labor processes in the production process cannot be synthesized or integrated into unified machine systems, then it will be technologically possible to disaggregate them out into specialized units of production. Second, if markets are fluctuating or unforeseeable, large firms may spin off certain activities (usually through subcontracting) in order to avoid the transmission of variability or uncertainty through the vertical structure of the firm. Third, if producers for final markets need inputs which can only be fabricated most efficiently by firms which are entirely dedicated to these inputs because of their firm-specific 'know-how', then they will shed these activities in order to take advantage of such know-how. Fourth, if these inputs can be made in factories whose minimal optimal scales of operation can only be attained if their production is marketed to a variety of downstream firms, costs of production will be less with disintegration.

---

[6] 'Vertical' refers to different operations within the chain of processes leading from the raw material to its transformation into a final output, whereas 'horizontal' refers to like operations. Thus, vertical disintegration is the fragmentation of different steps into separate production units, whereas horizontal disintegration is the establishment of multiple units performing similar functions.

Fifth, large firms with internal labor markets or with unionized labor forces often put out certain phases of the production process as an institutional strategy of avoiding positive overspill effects from their own labor relations and salaries systems to low-skilled workers. It is well known, for example, that in many Latin American cities extensive vertical linkages between formal and informal sector enterprises exist, analogous to relations between large and small firms in North American industrial systems (Holmes, 1986; Portes and Benton, 1984; Portes and Walton, 1981; Vieira da Cunha, 1983). Informal sector enterprises or small firms in industrial economies generally are often integral parts of the functioning of much larger industrial complexes, involving a diversity of firm types and a great deal of organizational flexibility. This description of the reasons for vertical disintegration is suggestive rather than inclusive, but it is nonetheless possible to understand that vertical disintegration is a common aspect of modern industrial production. It is neither a deviation from, nor strictly a precondition to, mass production or vertical integration (Bagnasco, 1977; Piore and Sabel, 1984; Storper and Christopherson, 1987).

Most relevant to the case of industrializing Third World nations, vertical and horizontal disintegration often arise as the organizational forms that production takes under the combined conditions of growth and uncertainty (and, in some ways the latter is a consequence of the former). As the extent of the market increases in an industry, it is frequently accompanied by shifting product designs or increasing product differentiation. As a result there are frequent incremental changes in production techniques, and fluctuating output levels. These conditions may be sectoral in origin—as in the rise of a new industry group—or macroeconomic—as in the advances and setbacks endemic to a developing (industrializing) economy—or they may be the result of conjunctural conditions, as in the period of macroeconomic instability experienced by most of the capitalist world in the 1970s and 1980s. Under any of these conditions, vertical and horizontal disintegration are used to achieve flexibility and specialization in industrial production, generally without reversion to low-productivity versions of artisanal techniques. Disintegration makes possible the realization of scale economies, but in the specific form of external economies (Scott, 1988a; Storper, 1989). The costs of production of the commodity at hand continue to fall as a result of specialization, but these economies do not come at the price of product and production process flexibility, since interfirm relationships may be changed as market conditions shift.

A deep social division of labor in a sector presumes the formation of an industrial complex. The complex is organized in terms of an elaborate structure of interfirm transactions, including the following types: (1) personal contacts; (2) exchanges of detailed information and coordination of strategies and product designs; (3) short-term and long-term subcontracting; and (4) circulation of inputs and outputs.

Frequently, these transactional relationships have geographically dependent cost structures. The greater the magnitude of these costs per unit of transactional activity, the greater will be the probability that firms will agglomerate in order to reduce them (Scott, 1988a). Three types of transactions especially affected by distance can be noted: (a) transactions that cannot be standardized—that is, which are unforeseeable—and which therefore require frequent search and renegotiation. This is the case in many industries where markets and product designs change frequently; (b) small-scale linkages that cannot enjoy volume discounts on transport costs; and (c) problematic linkages that must be resolved frequently through personal contacts or renegotiation. These factors will encourage spatial proximity of the partners in the relationship. All these types of distance-sensitive transactions are frequently encountered in vertically disintegrated production systems.

It is thus probable that complexes of economic activity with high levels of transactional activity will appear frequently on the landscapes of industrial economies (particularly capitalist economies because of the importance of economic competition and cost reduction in them). These agglomerated industrial complexes are simply *the geographical means according to which external economies of scale in production systems are realized by firms*.

Agglomerated industrial complexes are a principal basis for the rise of territorial growth centers, whose appearance on the landscape is often associated with the rise of new industries. For example, the contemporary electronics industry in the United States and Japan has a few definite centers of growth and technical innovation, such as Silicon Valley in California (Scott and Storper, 1987). Much of the history of industrialization itself is in fact the history of these geographically concentrated centers: automobiles in Detroit, textiles in Lancashire, firearms in Birmingham, cutting tools in Sheffield and Solingen, aircraft in Los Angeles, and so on. In Third World countries as well, industrialization efforts have yielded most of their results in the form of concentrated territorial growth centers. These industrial cities and regions arise as the social division of labor develops within industrial production systems, and not simply because these places furnish infrastructural inputs to industrial firms.[7]

There are additional endogenous sources of industrial agglomeration. As localized complexes of industrial production develop and grow, they draw into their spatial orbit a corresponding labor force which embodies within itself the basic skills and human attributes demanded by local employers. Diverse agglomeration economies flow from the concentration of many workers in one place, and these agglomeration economies help to

---

[7] This is the stock explanation of Third World urbanization in much of the literature.

underpin the overall pattern of localized growth. Two aspects of these economies can be highlighted.[8]

First, in any local labor market employers and workers both face significant search costs as they set about their respective tasks of filling vacancies and finding jobs. Firms in the industrial complexes I am describing—as contractors and subcontractors—experience a great deal of uncertainty. As such, they are likely to have rather high rates of labor turnover, in order to maintain their flexibility with respect to their markets (whether product markets or contractual intermediate output markets). For workers and employers, the larger and denser the local labor market, the more efficient a given investment in search activity tends to be. Finding and scanning activities are greatly facilitated where employers and workers are concentrated together in geographical space. In these circumstances, the subtle but important process of matching specific jobs to the characteristics of workers can proceed with maximum effectiveness (Storper and Scott, 1988b).

Second, and most relevant to the case of great industrial centers such as São Paulo, for any given rate of unemployment, large local labor markets by definition have a larger absolute pool of job seekers than small local labor markets. This implies directly that employers in the former type of labor market have a higher probability—in a given interval of time—of finding a job seeker with specified characteristics than employers in the latter type. This is all the more true if firms with high levels of output instability congregate in one area, since it produces a higher rate of demand for labor turnover in that local labor market. Accordingly, firms in large labor markets can adopt more flexible labor-turnover policies and externalize to a relatively high degree their labor-market relations; these possibilities allow them in turn to respond more effectively to economic fluctuations and uncertainties. The higher rate of labor turnover reproduces itself in large territorial labor markets because workers tend to find other jobs when released and thus they can remain in the labor force. Firms in small labor markets, by contrast, are more prone to hoard their workers because of the greater difficulties of finding replacements for vacancies when needed. In developed economies with high overall levels of labor absorption, this has led to the condition where new job openings in small local labor markets are relatively scarce. Jayet (1983) has formalized

[8] Thus, to reiterate, this concept of industrial complex is manifestly not the same as the planning concept. Input–output relations in the *static* sense are completely inadequate definitions of the industrial complex—both economically and spatially—because they cannot penetrate the developmental dynamics of the industry.

It is necessary to view the division of labor in a dynamic developmental context and thereby to understand which linkages will be geographically sensitive and which will not. The mere existence of interfirm connections is not in itself necessarily a sign that a territorial center will form out of an industrial complex, because routinized, standardized, and high-volume linkages can often be carried out at long distances.

these relationships with the observation that workers in urban areas tend to experience more frequent alternations of employment and unemployment, whereas workers in nonurban or small labor markets tend to experience more prolonged bouts of unemployment once they lose their jobs. We shall see later on that there are additional dynamics of large local labor markets specific to semi-industrialized countries which reinforce their advantages to employers (section 5.2).

The explanation of urbanization offered thus far, however, remains insufficiently dynamic and thus understates the interaction between the division of labor and urban industrial growth centers. Cities are not simply the necessary geographical expression of the growth of external economies in production; spatial concentration can also be a source of growth of industrial productivity. The developmental dynamic of industrialization is strongly attached to urbanization, because technical innovations in the course of development of leading sectors are frequently achieved within urban industrial complexes. This is because each center comprises a stock of organizational complexities, throwing into relief new technical and commercial possibilities. The very fluidity of organizational structures (interfirm relations, specializations, etc) creates a 'grid' of product and process opportunities. The people already involved in the daily life of each center are most capable of perceiving and taking advantage of these possibilities, in part because the whole system implies high levels of turnover and exchange of personnel as well as high levels of firm birth and death (Scott, 1988a; 1988b; Scott and Storper, 1987). Interfirm organizational complexities, combined with the labor-market structures of territorial growth centers, ensure that the territorial center will be the focus of technological innovations in products and processes, as is now the case in the electronics industry in Silicon Valley and the automobile complexes of Japan. These centers grow through processes of innovation and entrepreneurial activity. As a result, the division of labor is always on the move, regenerating new agglomerative impulses as old ones are retired through technological maturity or standardization. For example, in the contemporary microelectronics industry, basic inputs are both increasingly standardized and widely available, but intermediate inputs and final outputs are both increasingly differentiated and specific to each other, produced by specialized firms who can cope with relatively frequent product and process changeovers.

2.2 The urban hierarchy and industrialization
Industrial economies are not only urbanized; their cities are also arranged into hierarchies. Thus, all urban-industrial economies have an uneven geographical distribution of population and economic activity caused not only by urbanization, but also by the existence of an urban hierarchy. Polarization is associated with a highly uneven interregional distribution of population or activity in the form of a steep urban hierarchy.

We may ask why all industrial economies have urban hierarchies. Again, a disclaimer must be offered before proceeding: preindustrial economies also had urban hierarchies, often steeper than those in the era of industrialization, but for different reasons. I am only going to deal with urban hierarchies under the regime of industrialization.

This question can again be answered by reference to the division of labor in modern capitalist industry. Thus far, our analysis of the division of labor has treated the case of vertical relationships within a single sector. But the division of labor is much more complex than intrasectoral vertical relationships; it extends to the intersectoral division of labor in the economy as a whole. To capture this idea, think of each broad epoch of growth in the advanced capitalist economies: it tends to be associated with and based upon a particular *ensemble* of dominant production sectors. An ensemble is dominant when its component industries exhibit some or all of the following features: they employ large numbers of workers; they have unusually high rates of growth of output and/or employment; they have major propulsive effects on upstream sectors; they produce crucial capital goods or widely used consumption goods, where some or all of these goods have important repercussions on economic and social development. To drive this point home, I need only make reference to the textile age of capitalism in the early 19th century, the era of coal-steel-heavy industry at the turn of the present century, or the period of mass production dominated by automobiles and consumer durables industries in the decades stretching from approximately the 1920s to the 1960s. Now, we are entering a period dominated by new manufacturing industries such as electronics and new service sectors such as producer services (Scott and Storper, 1987). Each industrial ensemble tends to develop as an ensemble precisely because its individual industries have certain technological and intellectual complementarities, as in the continual spin-off of new specialty chemicals from the petrochemical revolution, or the input-output links between steel, electricity, and machine building, and the car and consumer durables sectors. These ensembles may share knowledge and innovative spin-off processes and they are often also highly connected at the level of production, because they depend on certain similar components or inputs, or because output specialization depends on economies of scale in provision of inputs which are then shared by a number of final output sectors. For example, metalworking or machining shops often provide inputs to a variety of final output industries. Machine tools are the 'heartland' technologies for a wide variety of production sectors in the durable goods industrial growth ensemble which dominated capitalist growth in the mid-20th century (Rosenberg, 1972). In the contemporary motion picture industry, firms that supply intermediate inputs are now marketing their outputs both to filmmaking and to television, causing a geographical relocation of television towards Los Angeles at the expense of New York

(Storper and Christopherson, 1987). Some interindustrial linkages, to be sure, may be amenable to routinization and thus can be realized at considerable distance; but many others encourage the formation of inter-sectoral industrial complexes, based around horizontal supplier linkages. These exist in addition to the intrasectoral industrial complexes described in the previous section.

Very large cities or industrial regions may appear in this process in two ways. On one hand, where any single sector is both highly agglomerated in space and very large in scale, it may generate a very large city. Big one-industry cities are common features of the capitalist industrial landscape, as in the cases of early 20th century Detroit and Pittsburgh. Neither of these developed into primate cities, because they developed in a country with many other large cities already in existence; both, however, were transformed rapidly from small towns into large cities and jumped up the urban size hierarchy in very little time. Ensembles may also take the form of a large growth region with a series of cities as was the case of the US Manufacturing Belt in the late 19th and early 20th centuries and is now the case of the US Sunbelt. On the other hand, a particular industrial ensemble may take the form of one very large industrial city and its immediate hinterland, as is the case in São Paulo, where one ensemble comprising metalworking, machining, and consumer durables, and another consisting of chemicals and pharmaceuticals have both concentrated into one very large city. In the USA, by contrast, each of these ensembles grew in a series of industrial cities and towns within different, regions, leading to a much more dispersed pattern of industrialization.

As with the case of localization economies for a single, vertically disintegrated sector, large polysectoral industrial cities enjoy economies of scale in the provision of infrastructure, the functioning of a large special-ized labor market, and so on. As a result, the growth of productivity in these cities often outstrips their counteracting diseconomies of agglomera-tion—especially in the period when the ensemble has many unstandardized or rapidly changing components. Generalized 'Verdoorn effects', or external economies of scale, come into being and allow the area's produc-tion system to keep outcompeting cheaper areas (Verdoorn, 1980). For example, it is often the case that in large cities the nominal price of labor is driven up by unionization or simply by pass-through of higher costs of living generally. At the same time, overall productivity is frequently higher, allowing capitalists still to enjoy a greater surplus product than if they were to locate in other regions; this is the classical, or Kaldorian, concept of regional efficiency wages. The existence of such a surplus for São Paulo has recently been confirmed empirically by Azzoni (1986; see also chapter 4).

Several additional points on the nature of the 'demand' for urbanization and urban–regional hierarchies now need to be made. First, Löschian market territories are more the outcome than the cause of urban hierarchies.

Given a certain level of market demand, each industry and ensemble is likely to establish its own organizational structure and linkage requirements, and thus its own market area. Moreover, although some urban or regional units are likely to be much larger than others, in a world of heterogeneous technologies and products it is extremely unlikely that these will assume the neat patterns envisioned by Lösch. The notion of strictly 'normal' hierarchies also rapidly loses its meaning, since a normal hierarchy in an industrial economy would have to presume that all the scale and scope relationships in the industries of different nations are identical to each other, and that the mix of products and income levels (and thus tastes and preferences) are also identical.

Second, there is no reason to expect stability in an urban hierarchy. Any modern industrial economy generates changes in its industrial mix and the associated social division of labor which may, in principle, create new complexes and thus new growth centers. As already noted, when new industry groups arise, their specialized complexes often have different locational requirements from those in existence in established centers. The locus of growth may therefore shift, leading to relative decline in older centers. But industrial dynamism may also renew growth in the very largest cities, notwithstanding their typically high factor prices, congestion, and well-developed political traditions. This is because, in all sectors of production, the temporal course of the division of labor is subject to dramatic and often unanticipated changes that break off new specialized functions even in these older industries.

To take one example, the cheapening of telecommunications and recent advances in information transmission have facilitated interconnection between firms and between firms and consumers in the producer services and banking industries. Some units of production have been enlarged, and their operations standardized as a result, leading to geographical decentralization (as in the case of 'back offices' in banking). But in a greater number of cases, intensified reagglomeration has occurred, leading to spectacular growth, as, for example, in the central city areas of New York, London, Los Angeles, Tokyo, and São Paulo. The ease of interconnection does not simply change the locational logic of a fixed set of activities—as most nondynamic locational theory would lead us to think—but it also acts to permit the development of new contours of the division of labor and thus to re-form locational needs. The revolution in electronic means of communication has thus not only failed to undermine processes of large-scale urbanization as was so frequently predicted in the literature of the 1960s and 1970s, it has actually led in many cases to considerable spatial reconcentration. This is because there is no definite end in principle to the interaction of scale and specialization in an industrial economy, and thus no reason to expect the end of agglomerative forces even with continued rapid improvements in transport and communications technologies.

Third, the development of the social division of labor even in older industries in older cities is not a one-way street. It is not simply the case that older industrial centers tend to lose their industrial activity automatically, as if dictated strictly by size and age of city. In some older sectors, there can be reversals in the process of standardization, engendering a return to a vertically disintegrated form of production organization after a period of vertical integration and decentralization. This is now occurring in the machine tool and motion picture industries in Japan, Europe, and the United States (Ohno, 1982; Piore and Sabel, 1984; Storper and Christopherson, 1987).

2.3 The division of labor, external economies, and economic theory

Before continuing our explanation of polarization, it is appropriate to take stock here of the nature and significance of the location theory outlined in the two previous sections. By comparing it with existing theories of agglomeration, we can gain a sense of its major differences from those theories.

Virtually all theories of polarization are premised on the idea that initial industrialization is made cheaper for an economy when industry is geographically concentrated, because the latter is associated with economies of scale. Agglomeration, though a central concept in urban and regional theory, actually refers to a number of quite different phenomena, none of which is easily measured directly (Azzoni, 1986). Agglomeration is said to derive variously from: economies of urbanization; economies of localization; and internal economies of scale of particular activities. Urbanization economies refers to the grouping together of different activities which then enjoy economies of scale in markets (as in central place theory), or urban infrastructure. Internal economies of scale in production—as when a given integrated production process is most efficient at a high level of output— also are associated with economies of urbanization in access to markets (if production must be close to final demand), and in the provision of infrastructure for large industrial units.

This analysis has centered on localization economies. Localization economies derive principally from intraindustry or interindustry specialization where greater scale of activity in the urban unit permits greater specialization among firms in their detailed functions and leads to the complex interconnections between firms as described above. Labor-market economies follow where size reduces employment search costs and allows firms to hire workers with specific skills or to adopt more flexible labor-quantity policies. Localization economies, in this account, are frequently associated with high rates of organizational and technological innovation, since these induce change in the technical and social divisions of labor in industry. It follows that urbanization economies arise in connection with the growth of localization economies; they are part of one historical process which is driven by the dynamic of production.

The essential differences between this view of the urban economy and that presented in conventional neoclassical urban economics is that the latter has little that permits an explanation of the *buildup* of large cities, except by reference to the exogenous creation of large scale in industrial production or urban infrastructure provision (as well as being focused on residential choice, not production). Typically, neoclassical urban economic models proceed from a set of givens about either economic activity or urban services and infrastructure, or both. They hold the 'demand' for various scales of agglomeration exogenous, asserting simply that much industrial activity enjoys higher productivity when spatially concentrated.[9] In practice, in the economic analysis of urbanization the structure of production is held constant, the costs of production are measured at different urban scales and with different industry mixes, and then partial equilibrium solutions to urbanization and location processes are worked out in the form of optimal or efficient patterns of spatial resource allocation. In the end, these exercises amount to the calculation of aggregate production functions for the city and its industries. These production functions are by definition based on *diminishing returns* for firms, a notion which is central to the neoclassical argument that, under conditions of competition, producers optimize quantities and prices. In neoclassical urban economics, there are indeed production function models that have increasing returns, but these returns are *strictly* the result of the scale of infrastructural inputs to private firms, and even here, such inputs ultimately are subject to diminishing returns. How, in this line of thinking, do firms go from one state of equilibrium to another (at a higher scale of operations)? How does the agglomeration/urban system as a whole manage to accompany these firms, if its infrastructural services as well as its firms are already in their equilibrium configuration?[10]

In this schema, all that is left to explain dynamic growth processes are exogenous factors such as population growth and technological change, which 'cause' firms and infrastructures to jump from one scale of operations

---

[9] It then follows that the 'problem' for the capitalist, the location analyst, and the urban planner is simply to match the scale of the 'demanding' activity to the scale of the 'supplying' infrastructure system, factor market, or consumer market, in search of the cost-minimizing and profit-maximizing location. With the aid of supercomputers and complex algorithms, transport costs can also be brought in as a proxy for spatial linkages.

[10] External economies are inconsistent with static partial or general equilibrium methods. Marshall recognized the existence of external economies and attempted to reconcile them with diminishing returns and thus to preserve neoclassical competition theory. But Sraffa (1926) showed this to be logically impossible. Thereafter ensued a long period in which the economics profession—with the notable exception of Young (1928)—simply buried the issue of external economies and its associated issue of the endogenous sources of long-run economic growth.

to another. In the domain of production, technology is the all-encompassing exogenous factor used to explain the residuals in the equations of the urban–economic models; but there is nothing that explains why technology changes. In effect, the standard analysis reduces the spatial–economic development process to a game of periodic reshuffling in the face of external shocks (technology and population) or gradual reshuffling in the face of spatial factor price changes.

There are two main analytical puzzles here. On the one hand, no sense is given of how the industrial development process gets launched in a place that lacks initial comparative advantage—undeveloped places may have the 'advantage' of cheap labor, but usually everything else (production costs at low scale of output, distance to markets, variety and quality of inputs, etc) drags down levels of productivity and thus drives up prices of outputs. How is comparative advantage *created* or built up in a place? On the other hand, the deus ex machina of technology makes urban scale dependent on technological indivisibilities in infrastructure, and yet it is clear that the size of many Third World urban industrial economies is much greater than what could be accounted for by such technological indivisibilities alone.

The creation of comparative advantage and the increasing returns to scale of industrial–urban complexes can only be fully accounted for by recourse to the notion of increasing returns to scale *in the production system itself* and in the specific form of *external economies* which are not just the result of size of infrastructure. Young (1928) called attention to the division of labor in production as the main source of these increasing returns. Capitalist growth is achieved through increasing the 'roundaboutness' of production, that is, through increasing interfirm and interindustry specialization, as well as increasing specialization within the technical division of labor in a specific firm. External economies thus arise as a consequence of the growth of output of a series of allied firms and industries. As Young put it:

"The mechanism of increasing returns is not to be discerned adequately by observing the effects of variation in the size of the individual firm or of a particular industry ... what is required is that industrial operations be seen as an interrelated whole" (1928, page 539).

For example, an increase in the demand for detergents may make the use of automatic packaging machines economical and thus reduce the cost of production not only of detergents but of the machines as well. The fall in the cost of the machines may make profitable their use in the making of corn flakes and cocoa, and so on. The similarities to Schumpeter's (1934) analysis of 'creative destruction' are obvious.

We can think of specialized (often smaller) industrial cities (that is, those whose economies are centered on one final output sector, vertically disintegrated) as well as diversified (usually larger) industrial cities (those with intersectoral production complexes, vertical and horizontal linkages) to be something like spatially extended industrial production systems. But a city is not like a firm, organizing the diverse elements of its production system under a managerial hierarchy; cities arise precisely because of the *social* nature of production in the form of the social division of labor.

It follows that neither the division of labor nor the space economy has the prospect of ever getting close to equilibrium.

"Every important advance in the organization of production alters the conditions of industrial activity and initiates responses elsewhere in the industrial structure which in turn have a further unsettling effect. Thus change becomes progressive and propagates itself in a cumulative way" (Young, 1928, page 533).

Moreover, with these true increasing returns, the techniques of production which are chosen (and thus, capital – labor ratios) are a function not of relative factor endowments and prices, but of the scale of production and the corresponding technological structure of the production process (Kaldor, 1972). Put more bluntly, technological development and choice are not guided principally by an effort to save on the most expensive factors of production, but by savings on total factor costs, or by improvements in quality. It follows directly, of course, that relative factor prices and the income distribution in a capitalist economy are not controlled by marginal productivities as in neoclassical reasoning. This would undoubtedly be the case with Young's external economies, but it has also recently been suggested as a condition which applies to any type of increasing return to scale, whether internal (technological) or external (the division of labor). The implication is that industries, as they grow and develop economies of scale, are capable of creating around them the preconditions of production, such as markets, factor markets, infrastructure, etc. They may do this by consistently paying 'more' for these resources than could be imagined from any equilibrium view, simply because productivity growth outstrips supply constraints over the long run, or because innovative firms and rapidly growing industries earn 'superprofits' (rents) which may be partially shared with their suppliers or their workforces. The problem of allocating scarce resources is reduced to secondary status. In terms of location theory, this means that the primary determinant of industry behavior in space—as well as in everything else—is not competition for scarce resources but technological and organizational development. This is a 'strong' view of capitalist competition based on these *developmental* forces rather than the 'weak' competition of the neoclassicals which is based on price-based *adjustments* (Storper and Walker, 1989, chapter 2).

Scale effects and their organizational form are the primary *direct* determinants of locational possibilities for they are the baseline determinants of production costs rather than factor prices (the mix of factors dominates the price of factors in determining production costs). If spatial price competition enters the picture, then, it is not as a basic determinant.

Conversely, location becomes important to industrialization not in its price-substitution effects, as claimed in conventional economic thought, upright but as a milieu in which the creative parts of economic processes flourish (and the working out of social – distributional relations as well; see chapter 5). Rather than viewing urbanization simply as a set of transactions *between* a given set of production activities and the environment, it can be seen that industrialization creates the urban environment endogenously, and can continue to keep doing so as long as the forces of production continue to develop.

The spatial division of production and polarization reversal

The framework which was presented in the previous chapter can be used to reinterpret the process of regional polarization in the course of industrialization, and to suggest how polarization reversal might come about. Remember that polarization reversal is defined as an interregional phenomenon where an economy begins to experience a fundamental weakening of the importance of its central region in favor of other regions. This would signify a reversal in the basic centralizing tendencies of the economy with respect to location patterns. I proceed by first telling a schematic theoretical story of polarization and polarization reversal in an industrializing Third World country, assuming the existence of importable technologies of production (section 3.1). Then, I clarify some of the finer points of the theory, distinguishing causal mechanisms from other interpretations found in the literature (section 3.2).

3.1 Growth and the spatial division of production

At the initiation of industrialization the extent of the national market for industrial goods of a given country is restricted in size. Only a small percentage of the population has the income required to consume most industrial goods. Because of this, economies of scale can only be realized in domestic production systems if industries are spatially concentrated, through the realization of external economies of scale.

This holds for a variety of industrialization strategies. In the country which begins by attracting foreign branch or assembly plants, for example, standard urbanization economies in the provision of urban services and infrastructure do encourage spatial polarization. Eventually, however, branch plants become easier to locate in peripheral locations, as the range of infrastructural services is extended over space. Yet polarization often persists in countries such as Brazil whose industrialization extends to the production of capital goods, and to a wide variety of industrial goods including not only traditional, products such as textiles, but also heavy industries and high technology. In all these cases, a very complex social division of labor is required and it usually takes a highly polarized urban and regional form, well beyond what is required or even desirable from the standpoint of urban infrastructure provision.

Once a given agglomerated industrial pole takes root at any specified regional location, its developmental trajectory then helps to consolidate that location as the privileged geographical focus of the emergent industrial economy. This latter state of affairs certainly seems to have been the case with São Paulo's rapid ascendance as the center of Brazil's modern industries, to the detriment of Rio de Janeiro. Whatever external economies Rio possessed earlier in the century were almost certainly associated with either state administrative activities or traditional industries; once

São Paulo gained an early advantage as the center of modern industry, Rio's fate was sealed. São Paulo emerged as a magnet for modern industries and subsequently grew via processes of vertical and horizontal disintegration, specialization, diversification, and externalization of the transactional structure of production (Cano, 1981; 1985; Townroe and Roseman, 1982). The whole became underpinned by urbanization economies that accrued from increasing efficiencies in infrastructural provision, and from the creation of a diversified and very large regional labor market suitable for modern industrial work. In no other Brazilian region did the processes of organizational proliferation and expansion of the production complex take place on such a scale or with such diversity. Once begun, the processes of organizational proliferation rapidly reduced the locational possibility set of subsequent producers, because of the increasing differences between the level of external economies of scale in São Paulo and these other places (see Cano, 1981; 1985).

As the industrialization and polarization described above are proceeding, the economy is experiencing sufficient aggregate growth and increases in per-capita income to cause the extent of the national market to grow and make possible an increasing scale of production of manufactured goods and to increase the potential specialization of the national industrial apparatus as well. Both of these processes open up possibilities for a reduction in the spatial polarization of industrial activity.

First, the existing ensemble of production industries may experience scale and organizational changes such that it begins to develop a more varied locational pattern. On one hand, existing industries may find that they can support production of an even greater proportion of their inputs domestically as a result of rising output levels. If the scale and specialization of these inputs is sufficient—or if these inputs can be fabricated as specialized outputs of an industrial complex which, through its own internal division of labor, adapts its outputs to serve a variety of final output industries—then a spin-off industrial complex may be able to come into existence, whose own localization economies dominate other locational forces. In this case, the locational pattern of the dominant ensemble may take the form of an extended industrial macroregion rather than a polarized industrial city-region. Moreover, even moderate levels of economic growth and income increases make possible the establishment of larger, more-capital-intensive plants, which may then take a more dispersed locational configuration owing to the large volume and standardized nature of their external transactions, whether with input-supplying plants upstream or markets downstream. Both these processes occurred historically in the American Midwest. A few dominant industrial cities developed (Detroit, Chicago, Pittsburgh, Cleveland) and numerous smaller subcomplexes eventually arose. Some plants were decentralized individually, first to smaller cities in the macroregion, eventually to other macroregions such as the Southeast and the West. The Midwest as a whole enjoyed significant 'regionalization economies', while each of its centers enjoyed urbanization and localization economies. As we shall see shortly, this may be—with lesser intensity—analogous to the case of São Paulo and southern Brazil since the mid-1970s.

However, it should be noted that branch and assembly plants located completely outside the polar region do not necessarily produce polarization reversal, for a number of reasons. Employment continues to be generated in the urban production centers of the existing ensembles, though at a decreasing rate because of the establishment of branch plants in peripheral regions. A spatial division of labor may thus be created, where different regions in the national territory specialize in functions within the vertical chain of operations of the production process. But the local linkages of far-flung assembly and branch plants remain minimal, their employment–output ratios tend to be low, and they only rarely lead dynamic innovation and spin-off processes (such as those I described in section 2.1). The pressure to centralize the most dynamic developmental processes in the existing industrial centers continues.

Fundamental alteration in the spatial locus of a nation's economic growth has historically been much more closely associated with the introduction or development of whole new industrial ensembles in the national economy. These industries frequently require inputs or resources that cannot be found in existing industrial complexes, particularly in innovative sectors, whose requirements are in general quite different from the inputs of older industries. New ensembles of production sectors enjoy a 'window of locational opportunity' because they are frequently relatively independent of the particular economies of agglomeration in existing industrial complexes (Scott and Storper, 1987). They create their own agglomeration economies endogenously as they grow, following the processes of vertical and horizontal disintegration described earlier.[11]

This shift in dominant ensembles may be a basis for interregional polarization reversal, and not simply for extension of the existing regional field of industrialization. Consider, for example, the way that different dominant ensembles were responsible for successive waves of polarization reversal in the United States. Beginning with the textile ensemble, industrial development was concentrated in a set of large and intermediate sized cities in the US Northeast. With the growth of the coal–steel–heavy industry ensemble, growth fundamentally shifted to the Midwest. Subsequently, the automobile and electrical machinery industries came to center on the upper Midwest/Great Lake regions. Even though the entire area from the

[11] Later, as these industries decentralize away from their own initial growth centers, their branch plants and subsidiary complexes may be located in different industrial peripheries from those used by their predecessor ensembles. Thus, they may be able to establish different regionalization economies from the industries that precede them, as has been the case in the recent development of the Sunbelt in the USA, the south of France, and the southeast of England.

Northeast to Chicago was called 'The Manufacturing Belt', in fact it was comprised of three different macroregions, developed in at least three distinct waves of industrialization, each organized around a different ensemble of dominant production sectors (see Pred, 1966). Most recently, the advent of a production ensemble based on high technology—electronics, aerospace, instruments, etc—has developed still another macroregion, the Sunbelt. The point is that each ensemble has the capability to alter dramatically the interregional spatial pattern of a nation's industry. Just as initial industrialization centers on a few locations and simultaneously excludes others, the addition of new industrial groups to the economy takes the form of 'concentrated dispersion' because it proceeds through the creation of new growth centers. Interregional polarization reversal is linked to continuing urban polarization.

This story of polarization reversal has rested on critical assumptions about the macroeconomic correlates of growth, of course. Specifically, it is necessary for income to rise, which then promotes increasing diversity of consumer and capital goods production in the economy. It is only with expectation of increasing markets that economies develop firms and entrepreneurial capabilities devoted to the innovation of new goods or, in the case of Third World economies, the implantation of an ever greater number of specialized production processes devoted to an ever greater number of products. In the view advanced here polarization reversal is essentially a consequence of *sectoral succession*. Spatially, this process mirrors the economic dynamic so aptly labelled by Schumpeter (1934) as a 'creative destruction'.

The polarized industrial city-region, such as São Paulo until 1975, can now be conceived as a special case of the development of territorial growth centers. Consider the locational effects of restrictions on the size of a national market, both in terms of an existing ensemble and in terms of the development of additional ensembles of production sectors. The smaller the extent of the market (here we are speaking of the effective market in terms of purchasing power, not simply population), the smaller will be the range of outputs of that economy, ceteris paribus. Its level of specialization as a whole will be reduced. In this case, there will be a restricted number of industrial complexes and territorial centers, and a steep urban hierarchy. Nations such as Brazil that start out with a relatively small effective demand have used industrial policies (such as import-substitution requirements) to telescope the sectoral diversification process in time. Nonetheless, if the overall scale of output of each sector thus installed remains moderate, various forms of *horizontal* (that is, inter-industrial) supplier linkages may develop to compensate for the size deficiencies of single sectors. To this must be added the inherent instability of many developing economies, which produces an extremely high level of fluctuations of demand and, thus, uncertainty for firms. This, too, will encourage an elaborate social division of labor, as for example when metalworking or machining shops provide inputs to multiple final output sectors, each of which may suffer considerable instability. In this case, many industries will tend to polarize together as a result of the social division of labor which is, in turn, the result of producers' strategies to minimize the risk that would be associated with vertical or horizontal integration.

The argument about polarization reversal may perhaps be clarified by way of a counterfactual scenario. São Paulo at one time dramatically changed the pre-existing pattern of Brazilian economic geography by stealing the mantle of production away from Rio de Janeiro. In its early stages, this resembled exactly the kind of 'polarization reversal by repolarization' referred to above. As we shall see in chapter 4, however, São Paulo ultimately continued to capture virtually all new industrial activity in Brazil for quite some time, while Rio suffered deindustrialization; São Paulo in effect simply recreated a polarized national industrial economy by entirely replacing Rio. For polarization reversal to take place, it would be necessary for polarization reversal by repolarization to be repeated a number of times over by different industrial sectors or ensembles of sectors: they would have to be newly introduced or grow to the point such that they could generate their own locational centers of gravity outside of the São Paulo region, and they would have to account for steadily increasing shares of national output and employment at the expense of São Paulo.

3.2 Polarization reversal by repolarization in context
At this point, it will be helpful to distinguish my notion of polarization reversal from other theories.

The comparative spatial development literature (see section 1.1) invokes a broad range of development processes which are supposed to lead to more even spatial development, summed up in the five bell curves (Alonso, 1980). Industrialization produces growth of output and income which, in turn, cause changes in fertility and relative factor prices (including wages), leading to a new geographical pattern of comparative advantage and, hence, to the decentralization of economic activity and the slowing of migration to the old center. Two basic processes are assumed in this complex reasoning: (a) industrialization leads to growth; and (b) industrial activity and population decentralize in response to changes in regionally differentiated factor prices, which are themselves a result of interregional differences in the level of development. For the moment, we can put aside the issue of whether industrialization and growth are necessarily related (we will take it up in chapter 5 in detail). Let us instead concentrate on the relationship between relative spatial factor prices and polarization reversal, since this is the heart of most urban and regional economics.

In the neoclassical view, firms must respond to changes in relative factor prices in the short run through substitution along a given production function. They do this either in situ, or by relocating (thereby substituting 'transport inputs' for other inputs). In the long run, for the neoclassical view to hold, technological change, that is, a change in production function, must reflect the frontiers of new factor prices and, in turn, locational behavior must be based on the set of new substitution possibilities thus created. This neoclassical view of locational change, like its view of agglomeration in the first place, is flawed because it does not have a realistic theory of production and its underlying technologies.

Assume the neoclassical short-run situation, where spatial factor prices are changing and technology is held constant. Factor prices and thus production costs rise in the industrial pole. This should always lead to relocation if transport-cost increases are not greater than the savings achieved through substitution. The old technique, in this view, could never 'come back'. Yet, as Robinson (1956) demonstrated, there can be no *unique* relationship between technique and factor price; one technique could be maximally profitable at two sets of prices. The extension of this logic to location suggests that there can be no *unique* relationship between spatial factor price changes and a given pattern of location (nor does it mean that firms are indifferent to factor price changes).

In the medium and long run, locational change is almost always effected through technological change. The question then becomes whether that technological change is induced by changes in the spatial pattern of factor prices. The answer must be negative, because technologies are packages of real machines, know-how, and organizational forms. Capital is not a fund of homogeneous and abstract value that engineers can shape, like putty, to minimize the use of the most expensive factors, at will. Indeed, technological changes are not generally motivated by the search to minimize the costs of a particular factor of production, but to exploit dynamic scale economies that result from the growth of effective demand and to make new things (new products) (Vieira da Cunha, 1983). The empirical evidence suggests that in the advanced economies the scale effect has indeed predominated over the factor prices effect (Pratten, 1971). The degree to which these scale effects are internal to a firm, or external (in the production system) varies, of course, but in any case they are of the dynamic type we referred to earlier (see section 2.3). The resulting ratios of factor demand have no equilibrium properties (Arthur, 1983; Kaldor, 1972; Nelson and Winter, 1982). As a result, even if industries attempt, ex post, to minimize their factor costs through their choices of locations, their range of possible responses will have little to do with the clean, smooth, unidirectional adjustments envisioned in conventional theories. It follows that, in the long run, industries' factor mixes are more important in determining location than the prices of these factors, and the mix is controlled by the technology of production of the industry at hand and of its backwardly linked supplier sectors. In the end, industries produce their own input histories through technological change (principally determined by scale and division of labor (Storper and Walker, 1989, chapters 2 and 3).

Take a concrete example of the implications of this reasoning. It is frequently wondered why the apparent diseconomies of agglomeration in large Third World industrial zones have not generated massive decentralization of industry, particularly in view of the fact that in many large cities infrastructure costs now often exhibit diseconomies of scale (Henderson, 1982). We frequently observe that large industrial centers have much higher nominal costs than smaller places, because of their traffic, pollution, infrastructure costs, and labor militancy, in addition to probable shortages of land and rising land rents. Conventional urban–economic models predict that these changes in relative factor prices between places will be sufficient to produce spatial decentralization of economic activity, first intraregional and later interregional, since industries will substitute cheap factors for expensive ones.

Yet, according to the reasoning advanced here, industries cannot simply flee their spatial growth centers at will. They must first liberate themselves from dependence on the agglomeration economies that exist in these industrial complexes. This freedom is mediated above all by various kinds of technological and organizational change, especially the kind that results in a streamlining of external transactions. Such change is principally dependent on the technology of production, which in turn is heavily linked to the scale of output. It does not come about necessarily in order to promote the industry's ability to use factors of production which are cheaper in other places; nor does it occur simply because such spatial price differences exist. The point is not that relative spatial factor prices are irrelevant, but that they are only a (small) part of causal explanation. It is probable that complex interactions between scale and scope in determining an industry's division of labor act to create *efficient* forms of production that may not, at first glance, appear to be correctly responding to the spatial pattern of factor prices. Much of the production efficiencies of large industrial regions can be attibuted to the vertical and horizontal linkages which exist between firms there. For many firms, moving away would require converting external economies which they enjoy to internal economies and thus assuming much higher levels of risk than currently exist in many production systems. Azzoni (1986), for example, has shown that São Paulo continues to enjoy enormous external economies of scale; that is, even though nominal wages in São Paulo are higher than in many other regions of Brazil, the difference between output values and wages remains greater there than in other places (thus wages are efficient in the Kaldorian sense). Moreover, it is probable that much of the productivity could not be found if the single plant or single firm were the unit of measurement. Thus, in measuring efficiencies it cannot be assumed that the 'industry' is equivalent to the production system.

Some additional observations on the nature of polarization reversal processes can now be made. First, Myrdal (1957) probably underestimated polarization reversal possibilities; he was pessimistic about the possibility that spread could ever overcome backwash effects. Like Kaldor, he tended to think of external economies as a function of the size of a place, rather than as *contingently* related to the size of a place through the organizational characteristics of its industrial production systems. His reasoning would have great difficulty in coming to grips with the contemporary reality of new growth centers in the USA outside of traditional industrial regions, as in the case of the electronics industry. Nor could he envision such a process ever occurring in the Third World. Yet, at least hypothetically, were the process of sectoral succession to take off in a Third World economy, then it would be possible for pieces of the system to break away from existing centers by exiting through the window of locational opportunity.

Second, any eventual process of reducing primacy will very likely not take the form of 'hierarchical filtering'. Hierarchical filtering has not occurred in the developed economies, nor is there any reason to expect it will occur in those now developing. Ensembles of dominant production sectors do not 'filter' down an urban hierarchy, but instead they locate in certain places selectively, by creating growth centers. Ultimately, they only decentralize from these centers selectively, creating their own growth peripheries. They may jump over or bypass some ranks in the urban system, while developing others. In the developed economies, indeed, industries have also jumped 'distances' with new ensembles locating their growth centers far outside of traditional industrial heartlands. So the possibility exists, in principle, for new complexes both to skip ranks in the urban hierarchy and to skip over territories (Storper and Walker, 1989). When a process of polarization reversal does finally occur in a Third World country, it is unlikely to follow a singular 'inflection point', after which all industry will smoothly and continuously shift out of the central region, since any putative process of developing other regions will very likely follow the uneven process of creating new sectors and building up their growth centers. In the balance, there may be a number of points at which the rates of growth of different places change, not one single switch: as we noted in section 2.2 the division of labor in a modern economy is subject to unanticipated changes and reversals. It may thus be capable of generating reconcentration in initial national centers after a period of diminishing regional polarization. Likewise, as was recently suggested in reference to the case of the South and West in the United States, polarization reversal does not have to stop at the point of regional convergence: new industrial regions might eventually become more highly developed than their predecessors, leaving the latter in a state of relative underdevelopment (Alonso and Medrich, 1978). More than anything, these dynamics are characterized by disequilibrium, change, and instability, rather than balance, rest, or evenness.

The case of metropolitan São Paulo: Latin America's largest industrial pole

4.1 Cidade Cinza (the grey city)

Speak to someone in Brazil of São Paulo, and the response will always be strong, if not uniform. Cariocas in Rio will without fault cite the absence of beaches and the 'southernness' (that is, work orientation) of São Paulo's culture, whereas those who come from the city or region of São Paulo itself will not only refer to the evident power of their region's economy and the cultural richness of the region but will even, on occasion, affectionately describe some of the city's renowned lack of physical charms[12].

The state of São Paulo was once dubbed Brazil's California by a leading business magazine, and the comparison is not inapt, for São Paulo combines the features of an extremely rich and modern agriculture and a diverse and large industrial economy, and in fact used the former to build the base for the latter, as was done in California (*Senhor*, 1986). Metropolitan São Paulo currently has the largest manufacturing economy of any similar region in Latin America, in terms of both employment and output, and accounts for about half of Brazil's industrial output. São Paulo has long served as a prime example of the horrors of polarization. More recently, a number of analysts and international institutions have argued that so-called 'polarization reversal' can now be observed there, for the first time in any major Third World industrializing economy (Richardson, 1980; Townroe and Keen, 1984). If, in fact, polarization reversal is occurring in São Paulo, it would be extremely significant from a theoretical standpoint. As such, São Paulo is an ideal case for scrutiny in light of the theoretical framework we have established in previous chapters.

Since most of the debate centers on the period after 1970, when polarization reversal is said to have begun, we will concentrate most of our efforts on analyzing the 1970s. First, however, a very brief historical background can be provided, for it suggests the ways in which São Paulo exemplifies some of the theoretical processes discussed earlier.

4.2 São Paulo's window of locational opportunity: 1900–1970

Viewed at the turn of the century, it would have been difficult to predict the rise of São Paulo as the principal industrial pole of Brazil. Rio de Janeiro possessed a commanding lead in this regard, with fully 44% of the country's industrial output. Rio was the national capital, the all-dominant center of Brazil's banking and trade operations, the location of the

---

[12] In the words of a song by the famous Brazilian composer and singer Caetano Veloso about São Paulo: "a dura poesia concreta de tuas esquinas ..." (the hard concrete poetry of your streetcorners).

country's major port, and the locus of its most skilled and diversified labor force. São Paulo was a secondary industrial center, with the vast bulk of its industrial activities devoted directly to the fabrication and servicing of its export-oriented coffee-producing agricultural economy, and the growing railroad network then being installed in the state of São Paulo to transport the coffee product to market.

Somewhere between 1907 and 1919, however, São Paulo overtook Rio as an industrial center, eventually leaving Rio in its current condition as a rapidly declining industrial backwater. No other state has come even remotely close to challenging São Paulo's industrial leadership in this century, none having ever again commanded even 10% of the nation's industrial output. Between 1919 and 1970, São Paulo's share of Brazil's industrial output climbed to its high point of just over 56% (table 4.1; figures 4.1 and 4.2).

The beginnings of *Paulistana* industrialization are fairly easily recognizable. The state of São Paulo became the coffee-producing center for the world in the early decades of the 20th century. The coffee economy supported a very rich agricultural bourgeoisie and generated enormous local capital resources, both in the private sector and, to a lesser extent, under state control (Brazil's government was very decentralized at that time). The *Paulistas* were forced to build a transportation system to get the coffee to market, resulting in the best regional transportation system in South America outside Buenos Aires. This accumulation of agrarian capital and servicing of the coffee economy induced some local industrialization, mostly in the form of machine-building and metalworking sectors. It also led to a derived consumer demand for industrial goods, some of which could be produced locally in São Paulo at an advantage over Rio, as they used nearby raw materials which could be delivered via the railroad system already developed for agriculture. The state became the first spatially integrated production–consumption system in Brazil.

Table 4.1. Value of industrial production by state (% of Brazil) (source: Conjuntura Económica **24**, July 1970, pp 89–106).

	São Paulo	Rio-Guanabara	Minas Gerais	Rio Grande do Sul	Remainder
1907	17	44	–	8	–
1919	32	28	–	5	–
1939	36	27	8	9	20
1947–51	46	21	6	8	15
1952–56	50	21	6	7	15
1957–61	53	18	6	7	16
1962–66	55	17	5	7	16
1967–70	56	17	7	6	14

Meanwhile, Rio's agricultural hinterland stagnated because of its exhausted soils and its traditional subsistence-based agrarian class structure that resisted conversion into the technologically modern *latifundista* structure that developed in São Paulo. In short, São Paulo began to benefit from two converging dynamics: on the one hand, a virtuous circle between industry and agriculture, much as once occurred in the agrarian Midwest of the USA, with the rise of railroads and the great machine builders there (Fishlow, 1965; Habbakuk, 1962); and on the other hand, an internally integrated space centered around the city of São Paulo which enjoyed a certain external spatial cost barrier permitting it to develop its own market independent of Rio.

This early historical trajectory helps us to understand São Paulo's initial ascent as an industrial power, but it is not sufficient to account for São Paulo's eventual extraordinary dominance over Rio nor Rio's continuing deindustrialization. The two major extant accounts of polarization in

Figure 4.1. Brazil: principal regions, states, cities (source: Instituto Brasileiro de Geografía e Estatística).

São Paulo are both flawed. The 'political' account of polarization holds that the centralization of political power in Brazil led to the centralization of industry. In this view, the agrarian bourgeoisie of São Paulo made itself largely independent of the banking and trading elites in Rio de Janeiro (Cano, 1981). This *Paulista* elite was able to marshal both the considerable

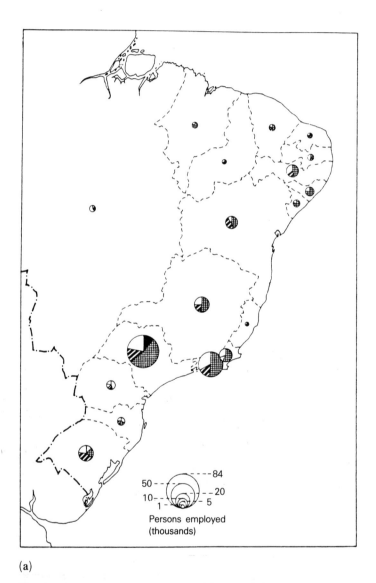

(a)

Figure 4.2. Industrial employment: (a) 1920, (b) 1970 (source: Instituto Brasileiro de Geografía e Estatística).

resources of the state of São Paulo, and more importantly—came to influence national policy. Beginning with the populist *Estado Nôvo* regime of Getúlio Vargas in the 1930s, so goes this story, national economic resources were increasingly directed to São Paulo, and the notion was affirmed that São Paulo and not Rio would become the national manufacturing

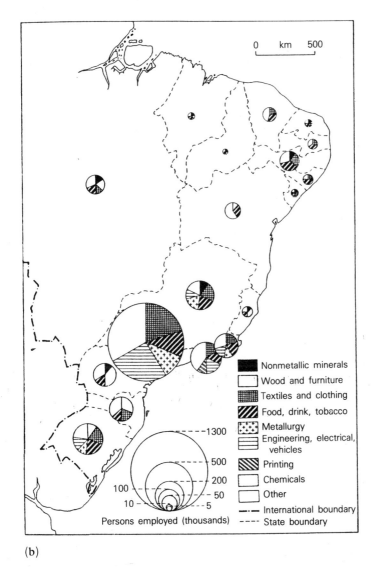

(b)

Figure 4.2 (continued)

center, serving not merely its own hinterland, but also national and perhaps international markets (Singer, 1977). But this account is contravened by most of the evidence, which suggests strongly that the Vargas regime favored Rio and not São Paulo. In the 1930s and early 1940s, headquarters of state enterprises were located in Rio de Janeiro and factories, wherever possible, in the state of Rio. These included the National Steel Company (1942), the Vale do Rio Dôce mining company (1942), the Volta Redonda steelworks, the National Motor Factory (1943), and others. Indeed, it was private investments that directed themselves toward São Paulo, not those of the state-owned companies (*estatáis*) (Geiger and Davidovich, 1986). Moreover, at the end of the Second World War, states recovered some of their autonomy as regional units, during the administrative reforms of the *Estado Nôvo*. As the federal government now relied on blocs of states to form ruling national political coalitions, it was required to satisfy a variety of regional interests. Although the national government increased infrastructure incentives in general, and much of these went to São Paulo, important geopolitical concessions entered into the distribution of resources, and in the Kubitschek administration of the 1950s, major industrial investments were made by the *estatáis* in the states of Minas Gerais, Rio, and elsewhere. Indeed, concern over the centralization of national population in Rio and São Paulo was so great that SUDENE, the Superintendency for Development of the Northeast, was created in 1959, in principle one of the most ambitious decentralization and regional development programs ever attempted. Not only was SUDENE an expression of the lack of monopoly of the Southeast in general and São Paulo in particular over the resources of the national government, but it also reflected the continuing importance of the class power of the rural elites based outside of the Southeast region (de Oliveira, 1977). The idea, then, that explicit national government policy or the class power of the *Paulista* elites produced the polarization of Brazilian industry in São Paulo is at best an extreme oversimplification.

A second competing explanation for São Paulo's ascendance is frequently proffered by economists. It may be summarized as follows:

" ... the public sector appeared committed to taking as many short cuts to its industrial modernization objectives as possible ... as a means by which to sidestep the high costs of an inadequate industrial environment, poor communication, poor transport links, poorly educated labor, inadequate power, by increasing the profits of particular sectors .... The São Paulo area—by heavily concentrating industrial activity—reduced the need for anticipatory physical and social infrastructure investments at any one time. In effect, it became an industrial city-state which could operate as a national center with only a fraction of the telephones, paved roads, power plants, and educational facilities needed to recreate the same type of environment at a hundred or a thousand other points in space" (Hamer, 1982, page 44)

As a statement of the logic of a strategy of spatial concentration, this quote is to the point; as a representation of the history of São Paulo, it is wrong, for the very reasons noted above. In the 1930s, national resources were centered on Rio, not on São Paulo, and in the postwar period, Brazil's administration of infrastructural improvements was strongly oriented toward building interregional political support through spatial *dispersion* of such resources. Many resources ended up being concentrated in São Paulo, but not because the national public sector willed that it be so. São Paulo's emergence as an 'industrial city-state' via the concentration of private power, private investment capital, and a local state powerful and rich enough to make public investments in the locality, remains unexplained by the standard economist's account.

Table 4.2 provides a clue as to why São Paulo was able to attain its success. The sectoral composition of the Brazilian economy underwent a dramatic change in the middle of the 20th century, with the traditional industries (often based on artisanal or semi-artisanal methods) which had once dominated the economy taking a back seat to the modern industries (here described as the dynamic A ensemble and the dynamic B ensemble, reflecting two waves of development and two sets of technical inter-relations). São Paulo attained a commanding lead in these industries in the 1930s, according to Cano (1981), and—as is obvious from table 4.3—held onto that lead securely as late as 1970. As well, many of the traditional industries began to be modernized and effectively transformed by the introduction of advanced machinery and modern factory methods (Vieira da Cunha, 1983). Many of these modernized units of production in traditional industries became highly dependent on access to the machine-building and machine-fixing capacities present in the other industrial ensembles, much as had occurred in New England's textile industry a century before (Hareven, 1978; Rosenberg, 1972).

Table 4.2. Sectoral composition of industrial activity (source: *Censo Industrial* IBGE, 1970; 1980).[a]

	Employment (% of Brazilian industry)				Output (% of Brazilian industry)[b]			
	1950	1970	1980	1984	1950	1970	1980	1984
Traditional	67.1	48.5	42.8	44.5	na	42.3	30.6	31.0
Dynamic A	26.0	30.7	30.3	28.9	na	36.0	45.2	48.9
Dynamic B	4.7	20.6	26.9	26.5	na	21.6	24.1	20.0
Total[b]	97.8	99.8	100.0	99.9	na	99.9	100.0	99.9

[a] When totals do not equal 100 it is because some sectors are not classified into one of the ensembles.

[b] na not available.

It can rather easily be surmised that a classical process of sectoral succession was at work in Brazil in the middle decades of the 20th century, and that the new or modernized industrial ensembles in Brazil, like their counterparts in other places and times, were relatively free from the agglomeration economies built up in old industrial centers such as Rio. At the same time, it is clear that a technology and skills base rooted in the metal-turning and metal-bending trades had begun to appear in São Paulo in connection with the industrial activities designed to serve agriculture there (Cano, 1981). Out of this technology and skills base, combined with rapid capital accumulation in the region, declining investment opportunities in coffee (soils exhaustion, downturn of world markets), and the constant infusion of relatively skilled immigrant workers from Europe (particularly Italy and Germany), a modern industrial economy could emerge. In short, the new industries took advantage of their window of locational opportunity to avoid Rio, and then they steadily built up their own, increasingly powerful, agglomeration economies in their own center of gravity, São Paulo. In contrast to explanations of Brazilian 'exceptionalism' rooted in the action of the Brazilian state, I would suggest that the process of polarization in Brazil was, if anything, the stock-in-trade of capitalist industrialization and its geography.

4.3 The 1970s: the economic miracle and its geography
The trend toward both relative and absolute polarization of Brazilian industrial employment and output up to 1970 changed somewhat shortly thereafter. During the 1970s, the São Paulo metropolitan area and the state no longer continued to increase their *shares* of Brazilian industry; yet, at the same time, differences in absolute gains in employment and output registered between São Paulo and the rest of the nation continued to grow dramatically. A number of researchers, principally associated with the National Spatial Policies in Brazil Project of the World Bank, claim that São Paulo's declining share of industry in the 1970s is evidence of 'polarization reversal', that is, that the theoretically postulated inflection point in the polarization curve is actually observable in Brazil in the early 1970s (Dillinger and Hamer, 1982; Richardson, 1980; Townroe and Roseman, 1982). What can we make of this claim? The decade of the 1970s was the period of the Brazilian 'economic miracle', in which annual growth rates were in the 8–10% range until the end of the decade (thus output and employment grew many times over), and in which massive new investments in physical plant and equipment were made in the Brazilian industrial economy. In terms of the theoretical argument presented in earlier chapters that polarization reversal, if it is to occur, will be based on growth in the scale of output and in the sectoral diversity of the economy (for these make it possible to deepen the division of labor and thus to separate firms and industrial complexes from each other without losses in efficiency), the 1970s are a good test case.

Table 4.3 shows São Paulo's share of industrial employment and output beginning in 1970. It appears that somewhere in the early 1970s, employment and output polarization in São Paulo reached peaks of about 49% and 57%, respectively. (Appendix A reveals that declines from these peaks began before 1975.) Notice, too, that the declines were most dramatic in the most rapidly growing ensemble, dynamic B. Appendix B provides a more subtle picture of São Paulo's relative decline in the form of a shift-share analysis of industrial employment, by sector and by sectoral ensemble, for the principal industrial states of Brazil. It reveals clearly that, in relative terms, there was an across-the-board negative shift for São Paulo and positive shifts in the remaining major industrial states, with the exception of Rio, which continued its historic slide (see also Diniz and Lemos, 1986).

Table 4.3. São Paulo's share (%) of Brazilian industry (source: *Censo Industrial* IBGE, 1970; 1980).

	Employment			Value of output		
	1970	1980	1984	1970	1980	1984
Traditional	42.3	38.4	37.1	49.6	44.0	44.5
Dynamic A	51.9	48.0	49.0	53.5	50.8	49.7
Dynamic B	69.2	62.4	63.2	77.3	69.4	69.9
All industry	48.9	46.3	47.5	57.0	53.2	52.1

When we examine the absolute growth and location of manufacturing employment and output in the 1970s, however, a different impression emerges. Table 4.4 ranks the magnitude of change for a number of different indicators of the performance of the industrial economies of the leading industrial states of Brazil during the 1970s. On the first three indicators—which measure increases in the volume of output in different ways—São Paulo ranks first in every instance for every industrial ensemble, and the differences between São Paulo and the second ranked growth area are, in every instance, enormous. To confirm the significance of these figures, Table 4.5 gives the resulting difference in manufacturing employment between São Paulo and the next three largest and fastest-growing industrial states for 1970 and 1980. In every case, São Paulo's margin of difference grows considerably. For example, whereas in 1970 São Paulo had about 1 million more industrial workers than Rio Grande do Sul, in 1980—despite the negative picture implied by the shift-share analysis—São Paulo had about 1.8 million more industrial workers than Rio Grande do Sul.

Table 4.4. Rankings of the magnitude of change for a number of different indicators of the performance of the industrial economies of the leading industrial states of Brazil, 1970–80.

	Rank[a]					
	1	2	3	4	5	6
(a) *Absolute change, all industry*						
Employment (workers)	SP 989301	RGS 238795	MG 202067	SC 153576	PR 119904	RGB 119363
Output (1000 $Cr)	SP 154413959	RGB 26877515	MG 26684762	RGS 22211759	PR 16956807	SC 13441722
Value added (1000 $Cr)	SP 60398194	RGB 9783541	MG 9741420	RGS 9065292	PR 5791894	SC 5702050
Plant size (workers)	RGS 11.50	SP 11.12	SC 10.98	RGB 6.48	PR 6.22	MG 6.12
Employment (%)	SC 135.58	RGS 109.76	MG 108.43	PR 107.08	SP 76.74	RGB 33.43
Output[b] (1000 $Cr)	PR 53.44	SP 45.75	MG 45.25	RGB 44.20	SC 35.96	RGS 29.70
Value added[b] (1000 $Cr)	PR 2.73	SC 2.10	RGB 1.51	RGS 1.15	SP 1.06	MG 0.45
Wages[b] (1000 $Cr)	MG 2.49	SP 1.91	RGS 1.38	SC 1.33	PR 1.21	RGB 1.11
(b) *Absolute change, traditional sector*						
Employment (workers)	SP 228190	RGS 119537	SC 65043	MG 57895	PR 39208	RGB 23968
Output (1000 $Cr)	SP 29966539	RGS 8492466	RGB 7301270	SC 6404006	MG 6343695	PR 4499738
Value added (1000 $Cr)	SP 11175245	RGS 3588885	RGB 2815703	SC 2387265	MG 2071779	PR 1389322
Plant size (workers)	RGS 13.86	SC 13.45	SP 6.76	PR 5.38	MG 4.74	RGB 2.40
Employment (%)	SC 138.79	RGS 104.96	PR 103.54	MG 62.03	SP 46.26	RGB 14.19
Output[b] (1000 $Cr)	SC 41.36	RGB 33.50	MG 28.32	PR 28.29	SP 26.82	RGS 17.51
Value added[b] (1000 $Cr)	SC 2.22	RGB 2.12	PR 1.46	SP 1.35	RGS 1.25	MG 0.91
Wages[b] (1000 $Cr)	SC 1.27	MG 1.11	RGS 0.70	SP 0.59	RGB 0.58	PR 0.50

Table 4.4 (continued)

	Rank[a]					
	1	2	3	4	5	6
(c) *Absolute change, dynamic A industries*						
Employment	SP	MG	RGS	RGB	SC	PR
(workers)	255 299	74 464	45 943	35 639	33 379	29 528
Output	SP	RGB	MG	PR	RGS	SC
(1000 $Cr)	69 026 930	15 931 469	15 060 402	8 992 286	8 899 447	3 241 771
Value added	SP	MG	RGB	RGS	PR	SC
(1000 $Cr)	23 777 071	4 989 073	4 270 763	2 838 615	2 738 053	1 363 898
Plant size	SC	SP	RGB	RGS	PR	MG
(workers)	8.37	7.40	5.79	5.04	3.05	1.74
Employment	SC	MG	PR	RGS	SP	RGB
(%)	148.99	117.54	110.13	88.24	66.62	39.55
Output[b]	PR	RGB	SP	MG	SC	RGS
(1000 $Cr)	141.07	105.18	86.13	72.10	45.27	−121.22
Value added[b]	PR	RGB	SC	SP	RGS	MG
(1000 $Cr)	7.51	2.91	2.73	12.22	2.21	0.88
Wages[b]	MG	SP	RGS	SC	PR	RGB
(1000 $Cr)	2.32	1.87	1.68	1.33	1.28	0.83
(d) *Absolute change, dynamic B industries*						
Employment	SP	RGS	MG	RGB	PR	SC
(workers)	393 532	55 131	53 633	52 350	28 080	25 260
Output	SP	RGB	MG	RGS	SC	PR
(1000 $Cr)	47 442 290	5 691 319	4 397 176	3 483 998	2 353 025	1 642 611
Value added	SP	RGB	MG	RGS	SC	PR
(1000 $Cr)	20 913 271	3 239 483	2 256 564	1 906 990	1 123 318	751 142
Plant size	MG	RGS	RGB	SP	PR	SC
(workers)	37.94	32.60	29.44	19.55	16.41	15.76
Employment	PR	MG	SC	RGS	SP	RGB
(%)	350.08	262.17	223.46	196.74	114.50	78.31
Output[b]	MG	SC	SP	RGB	PR	RGS
(1000 $Cr)	42.14	39.44	36.01	28.73	24.73	19.74
Value added[b]	MG	SC	RGB	SP	RGS	PR
(1000 $Cr)	1.01	0.71	0.60	0.53	0.14	−0.21
Wages[b]	MG	RGB	PR	SC	SP	RGS
(1000 $Cr)	3.79	3.02	2.76	2.69	2.56	2.54

[a] MG Minas Gerais; PR Paraná; RGB Rio-Guanabara; RGS Rio Grande do Sul; RJ Rio de Janeiro; SC Santa Catarina; SP São Paulo.

[b] These are values per worker.

How do we arbitrate between these two different statistical perspectives? From the standpoint of the theory of agglomeration, of course, it is absolute size and absolute growth that suggest the existence of external economies. Polarization, on the other hand, necessarily refers to the relative sizes of places. The relevant question, as it was posed in chapter 1, is the nature of the *process* of geographical industrialization; hence, what we are really interested in finding out by way of examining the recent spatial history of Brazil is whether the relative decline of São Paulo in the 1970s is a sign that a process has begun which will significantly reduce the level of spatial polarization of industrial activity in the Brazilian territory.

This question can in part be answered by way of historical analogy, considering the earlier process of polarization reversal in the United States. New York rose to prominence as the premier industrial pole of the United States in the middle of the 19th century, on the basis of an ensemble of 'traditional' industries such as apparel, leatherworking, printing, and small-scale machine building (Lampard, 1986). As early as the 1870s a series of Midwestern cities such as Detroit and Chicago had growth rates greater than that of New York, but these created virtually no perceptible threat to New York's status as the manufacturing center of the USA in the last three decades of the 19th century: by the end of the century, indeed, New York's absolute lead over these places was greater than it had been in 1870. With the takeoff of a new industrial ensemble based on the automobile and technologically cognate machine-building sectors around the first decade of the 20th century, manufacturing employment began to increase—in absolute terms this time—more rapidly elsewhere than in New York and the Mid-Atlantic region and the industrial polarization of the US economy began to diminish. Even with this reversal of growth rates, however, New York remained the largest US manufacturing center in absolute terms well into the 1950s. It was not until New York underwent an absolute decline in its manufacturing employment that it ceased to be the country's largest industrial pole.

Several lessons are apparent from this quick sketch. First, polarization reversal by repolarization of industrial activity—as in the development of industrial cities of the US Midwest after the initial industrialization of New England and the Mid-Atlantic regions—occurs as new industrial ensembles are installed and grow rapidly and to a very large scale. Second, even this

Table 4.5. Differences between employment level in São Paulo and other states, in absolute terms, 1970–80 (source: *Censo Industrial* IBGE, 1970; 1980).

	1970	1980
São Paulo–Rio Grande do Sul	1 071 524	1 822 030
São Paulo–Minas Gerais	1 102 722	1 889 956
São Paulo–Paraná	1 177 103	2 046 500

growth has only limited effects on overall patterns of spatial dominance, since there are often powerful feedbacks between already-industrialized regions and new industrial complexes [input–output linkages of all sorts (see Pred, 1977)]. Third, dramatic reversal of such patterns of polarization occurs when old industrialized areas decline while, simultaneously, new industrial ensembles grow rapidly in new territorial centers; it is the latter combination that has recently enabled Los Angeles to become the largest US manufacturing region at the expense of New York, and which has enabled the US South and Southwest generally to exceed the manufacturing output and employment of the North. If we take polarization reversal to refer to a definite result, in the sense of an eventual pattern of spatial development where other centers equal to São Paulo come into existence, then what are needed are major shifts in patterns of absolute growth and absolute decline. The evidence for Brazil presented here does not suggest any such pattern of reversal, unless we make the heroic assumption that the marginal shifts in shares we have observed will continue unperturbed so as to culminate in a more even pattern of development in the 21st century (we shall see shortly that the patterns of the 1970s have already been perturbed).

4.4 The 1970s reconsidered

This rejection of the notion that a definitive point of polarization reversal has been reached leaves open an explanation of what did happen to produce the shifts in shares of the 1970s. Did the growing dynamic A and B ensembles enjoy rapid scale increases which permitted the elaboration of the division of labor within their production systems and thus the installation of some plants outside São Paulo? State policy was certainly used to encourage such moves; in the dynamic B sector, for example, Fiat located its assembly plant in the state of Minas Gerais with the aid of considerable state subsidies, while in the dynamic A ensemble, the Brazilian government built a massive petrochemical complex at Camacari in the state of Bahia. With the generalization of industrial infrastructure, particularly in the developed Southern and Southeastern states, it became progressively easier to locate branch or assembly plants either in these states, or in the state of São Paulo but outside the immediate metropolitan area.

Before turning again to the data, let us remind ourselves of the two alternative theoretical perspectives which were presented and criticized in previous chapters. The conventional theory would explain a reduction in polarization as a locational response to a change in the spatial pattern of relative factor costs. Hence, industrial investment shifts to peripheral areas as a way to minimize the costs of production and this short-term behavior ultimately has efficiency-maximizing properties for the economy as a whole. The more classical perspective, on the other hand, suggests outcomes quite different from those of the neoclassical theory. Because of the existence of scale economies in the form of Verdoorn effects, productivity growth in large centers frequently outstrips wage growth, continually recreating a large 'producer's surplus', in spite of the growth of nominal factor costs. Thus, where one theory predicts decentralization in response to the geographical pattern of factor prices, the other predicts that the opposite will frequently hold. Our framework, it can now be seen, incorporates the predictions of both these theories by attempting to comprehend the development of industrial systems as technologically complex assemblages of techniques, organizations, and social practices which define, at any given moment, the underlying locational possibilities of the units of the system. Thus, it is to be expected that: (a) Production systems in large urban areas will often manifest external economies that permit them to support higher nominal factor prices than are available in

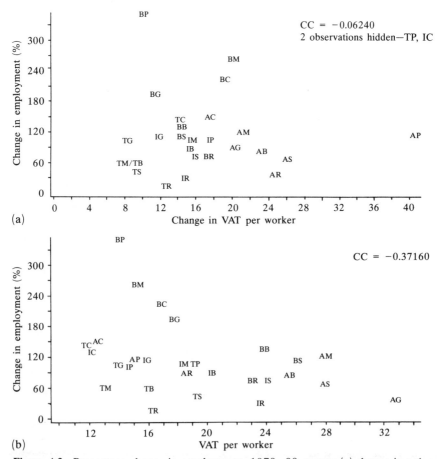

Figure 4.3. Percentage change in employment, 1970–80, versus (a) change in value added per worker, 1970–80; (b) value added per worker, 1970; (c) value added divided by wages, 1970; (d) value added per worker minus wage per worker, 1970.

peripheral areas without any loss in efficiency. (b) Production units will not smoothly and automatically move to cheaper peripheral areas even when factor cost differences are great, since such movement frequently depends on scale and scope changes in the production process which permit effective linkage over great distances, and these are not always available or economically efficient; production units may find themselves spatially 'trapped'. (c) Conversely, production units may 'opportunistically' move to cheaper areas even when productivity increases faster than factor costs in existing locations: where scale and scope changes permit effective long-distance linkage, producers may (especially under harshly competitive

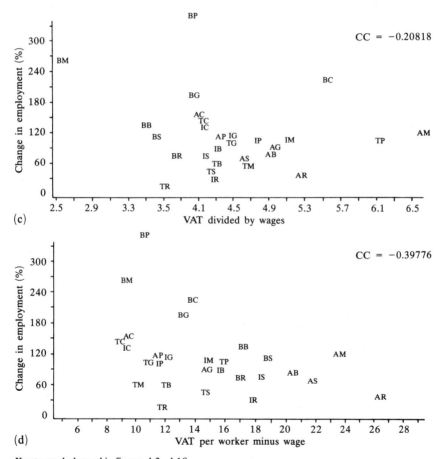

Key to symbols used in figures 4.3 – 4.18

The first letter refers to type of industry: A dynamic-A industries, B dynamic-B industries, I all industry, T traditional industries.The second letter refers to the region: B Brazil, C Santa Catarina, G Rio Grande do Sul, M Minas Gerais, P Paraná, R Rio de Janeiro State, S São Paulo State. CC is the correlation coefficient.

Figure 4.3 (continued)

conditions) abandon central industrial zones. In other words, the geographical responses to factor costs are always mediated by the complex technological and organizational nature of the production system in question, as it imposes constraints and creates possibilities for locational decisions.

The evidence on the spatial development of the Brazilian industrial system in the 1970s suggests that all three of these dynamics were at work, rather than one simple process of concentration or polarization reversal. A wide variety of calculations were carried out, based on the Brazilian industrial censuses of 1970 and 1980, the raw data for which may be found in appendix C. The basic method for each exercise was to correlate two variables, using as the units of observation the values assumed by those variables for particular industrial ensembles in the major industrial states of Brazil (with the exception of the values for all Brazilian industry, which are also plotted). The correlation coefficients thus express the degree of similarity or difference between places and industry groups. To be sure that we do not attribute differences between industry groups to differences between states, the variables are plotted for each group and one can examine the individual cases.

Figure 4.3 provides some indirect indicators of the relationship between productivity and locational change. Employment changes are plotted against different potential measures of productivity, with the assumption that differential productivity opportunities lie behind investment behavior. Note that there is virtually no relationship between changes in employment in different places and the change in value added per worker in the decade under examination. Moreover, the sign is actually negative (though the coefficients are not all that high) when we examine three other indirect indicators of the productivity of labor: (1) the value added per worker in 1970; (2) the ratio of value added to the wage bill in 1970; and (3) surplus of value added per worker over the wage paid per worker in 1970 (see also table 4.7, which is discussed later on). In other words, it does not seem to be the case that the existence of productivity differentials between places alone can account for geographical patterns of industrial change, as would be expected from the Kaldorian theory.

Nor does the existence of lower wages in the peripheral areas seem to be capable of accounting for locational changes observed, as would be expected from the neoclassical line of explanation. Figure 4.4(a) shows the average wage in 1970 and change in employment in the 1970s, and there is virtually no correlation between the two. On the contrary, as figures 4.4(b), 4.4(c), 4.5, and 4.6(a) suggest, changes in wages are themselves functions of investment and employment creation in the locality, rather than the other way around. Indeed, it seems much more likely that wages in industrial São Paulo, though higher than in nonindustrialized areas, represent a certain bare minimum for insuring a reliable workforce, and that this basic nonindustrial wage – industrial wage difference is almost immediately replicated in localities where modern industry installs itself.

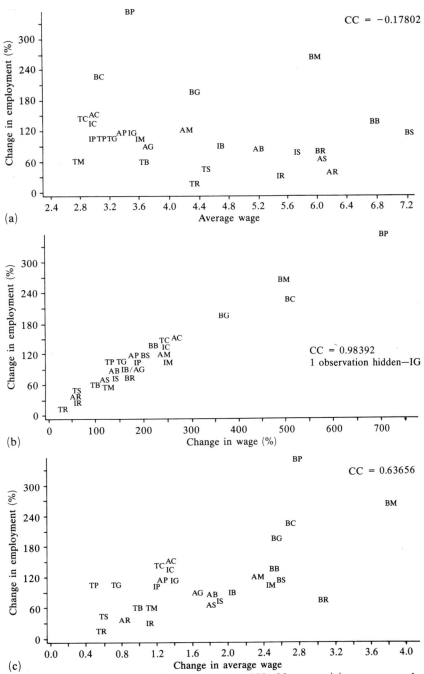

Figure 4.4. Percentage change in employment, 1970–80, versus (a) wage per worker, 1970; (b) percentage change in wages, 1970–80; (c) change in wage per worker, 1970–80.

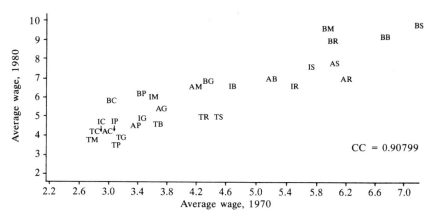

Figure 4.5. Average wage per worker, 1980, versus average wage per worker, 1970.

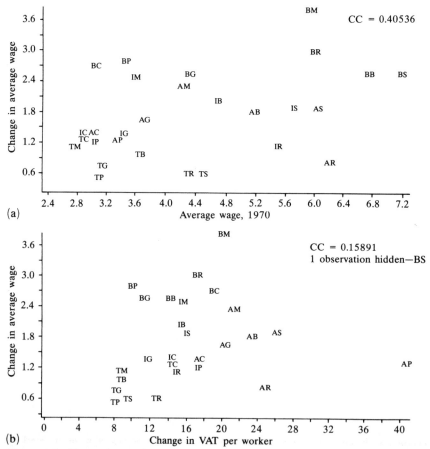

Figure 4.6. Change in average wage per worker, 1970–80, versus (a) average wage per worker, 1970, (b) change in value added per worker, 1970–80.

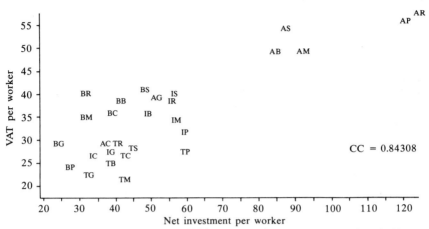

Figure 4.7. Value added per worker, 1980, versus net investment per worker, 1980.

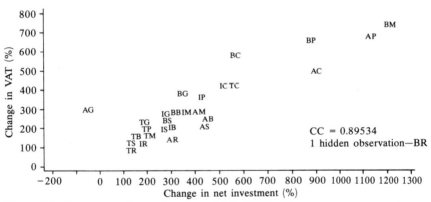

Figure 4.8. Percentage change in value added, 1970–80, versus percentage change in net investment, 1970–80.

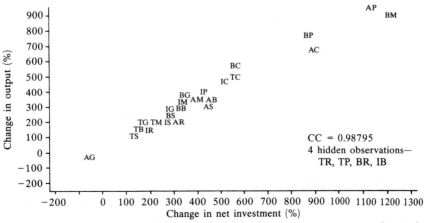

Figure 4.9. Percentage change in output, 1970–80, versus percentage change in net investment, 1970–80.

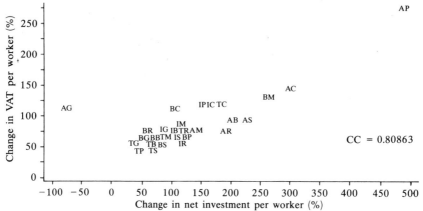

Figure 4.10. Percentage change in value added per worker, 1970–80, versus percentage change in net investment per worker, 1970–80.

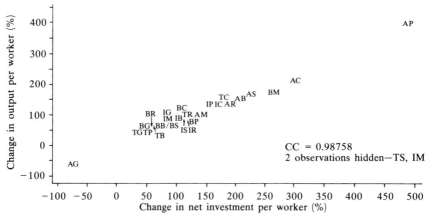

Figure 4.11. Percentage change in output per worker, 1970–80, versus percentage change in net investment per worker, 1970–80.

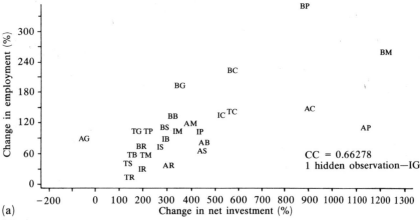

(a)

Figure 4.12. Percentage change in employment, 1970–80, versus: (a) percentage change in net investment, 1970–80; (b) percentage change in average plant size, 1970–80; (c) percentage change in number of plants, 1970–80; (d) percentage change in output, 1970–80.

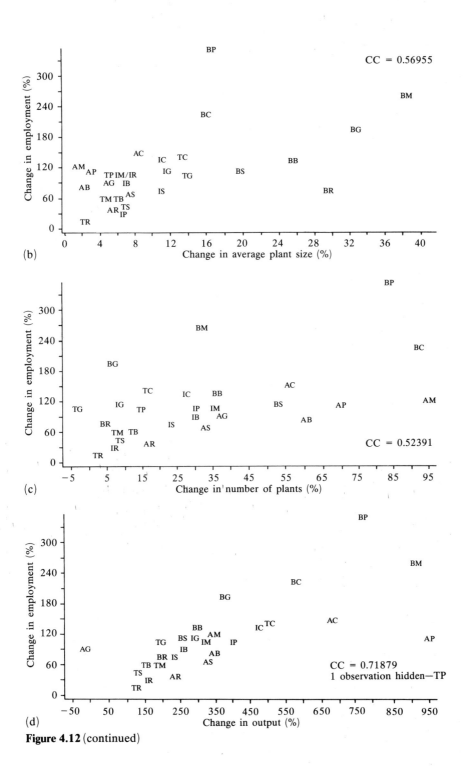

Figure 4.12 (continued)

Thus for plants of similar sizes and in similar industries, wages converge rapidly in spite of the vast differences in size and history of the labor markets involved; there is labor surplus everywhere in Brazil which establishes and holds this industrial wage rate where it is (Storper, 1984; see chapter 5 for a more detailed treatment of this issue). To make the puzzle even more complex, we can observe that changes in local wage levels do not appear to be a function of productivity changes per se [figure 4.6(b)].

Even though local productivity changes are not clearly functions of the local wage or labor exploitation structure, those productivity changes are systematically related to the quantity of investment, that is, the extent to which capitalists presumably made an effort to restructure or intensify the use of capital in the local industrial production apparatus (figures 4.7 – 4.11). The question then becomes, what systematically accounts for the spatial investment behavior of capitalists, if it is not either factor prices or pre-existing productivity characteristics of different localities?

What is missing in both the Kaldorian and the neoclassical accounts, of course, is a sense of technological and organizational heterogeneity, and the way it shapes locational behavior. Figure 4.12 plots changes in employment against changes in investment, plant size, number of plants, and output. Although the correlation coefficients are all over 0.5, they nonetheless express a considerable range of changes in employment for a given change in one of the other variables, suggesting in turn that investments in different places but within industry groups manifest significant technological heterogeneity; one has only to look at the values of the variables which describe the technical structure of production [in appendix C and table 4.6(a), see below] to see that they remain quite different within ensembles and between places.

Likewise, it appears that the state of the local labor market is a poor predictor of industrial location decisions or aggregate industrial growth trends. Figures 4.13 and 4.14 are analyses of two different ways of approximating the exploitation of labor. In the first, the overall ratio of value added to wages in each ensemble and locality in 1970 is plotted against its value for 1980, and it can be seen that the earlier value does not control the later value. The result is almost identical when the values per worker are examined. It appears that the different technological and organizational characteristics of each group of industries brings with it differential *opportunities* for the developmental trajectory of the exploitation of labor in the locality. Figures 4.15 and 4.16 suggest that plant size is not as good a proxy for the technological characteristics of an industry (which underlie its productivity levels) as we might think: putting aside the correlation coefficients (which in this case are not helpful because they do not hold constant the different mixes of industries in different places), we can see that physical or economic labor productivity for each group of industries is roughly in the same range for each state, but that plant sizes differ widely for the same productivity levels.

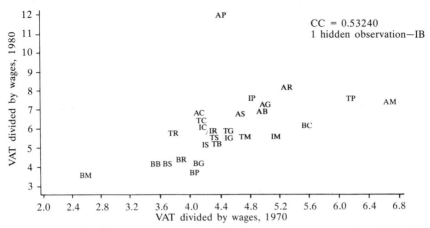

Figure 4.13. Value added divided by wages, 1980, versus value added divided by wages, 1970.

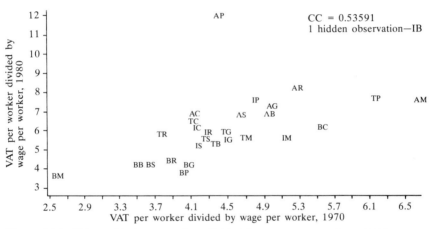

Figure 4.14. Value added per worker divided by wage per worker, 1980, versus value added per worker divided by wage per worker, 1970.

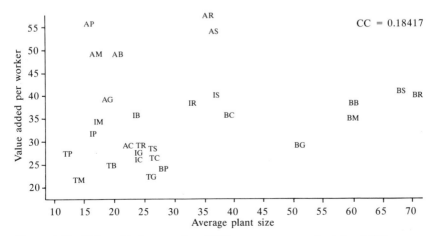

Figure 4.15. Value added per worker, 1980, versus average plant size, 1980.

Is there a role for the wage rate, if not for some general 'productivity' of labor? We have already seen that *average* wages tended to converge over the decade between places. Figures 4.17–4.18 show clearly that the main factor controlling wages is plant size, no matter what the industrial group or the location (but remember that even so, plant size is not a good predictor of labor productivity). Clearly technologically heterogeneous local industrial growth is strongly behind the evolution of local wages and the latter is not particularly tied to the pre-existing characteristics of the local labor market. In the end, industry mix and specific technological–organizational characteristics make local productivity, and plant size makes the local wage rate. The two are relatively independent of each other.

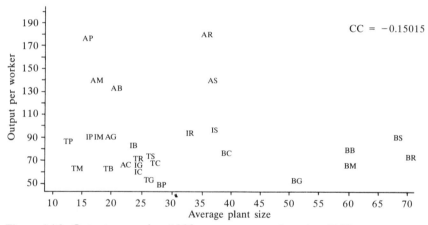

Figure 4.16. Output per worker, 1980, versus average plant size, 1980.

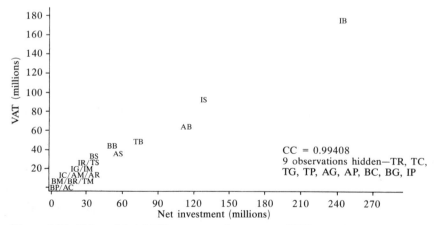

Figure 4.17. Value added, 1980, versus net investment, 1980.

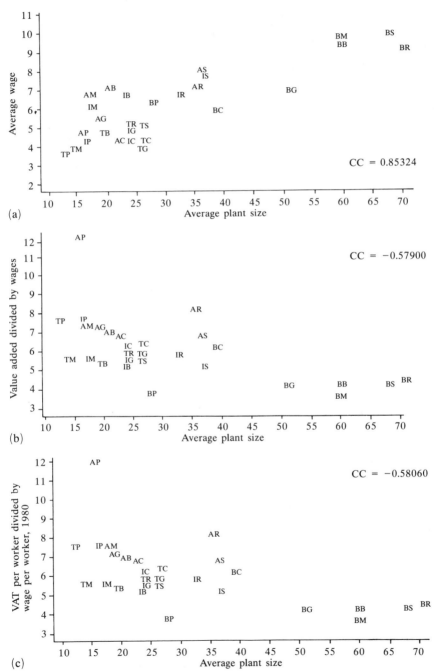

Figure 4.18. (a) Wage per worker, 1980; (b) value added divided by wages, 1980; (c) value added per worker divided by wage per worker, 1980 versus average plant size, 1980.

4.4.1 The situation state-by-state

Table 4.6 provides a resume of the characteristics of the industrial system in each of the main industrial states of Brazil outside of São Paulo. We can make certain reasoned guesses about the development of industry in each state during the 1970s based on this information. It appears that a differential mix of three phenomena was operative in each state in the 1970s: (a) location of large modern branch plants of *Paulista* industries or of the *estataís* (state-owned companies); (b) in situ modernization of pre-existing traditional industries; and (c) growth of local industrial complexes in the dynamic sectors, largely independent of those sectors in São Paulo.

Minas Gerais has a large and rapidly growing, fairly diversified industrial economy. We observe a number of different trends. The traditional sector did not grow very rapidly and appears to have undergone little modernization: it retains very small plants and very low wages. The dynamic A sector, on the other hand, grew quite fast; it has very small plants, but moderate wage levels and quite high worker productivity, giving it a fairly high level of worker exploitation. Much of the dynamic A sector is, in fact, located in the Sul de Minas region (the part of the state of Minas Gerais which comes very close to São Paulo), which is within the orbit of metropolitan São Paulo (Azzoni, 1986) (see figure 4.19). What this means is that many of these plants are probably linked into the São Paulo dynamic A sector, which explains their small size but high productivity. The dynamic B sector in Minas, however, grew extremely rapidly, and shows large plants and very high wages. There is a simple explanation for this growth: Fiat located a major assembly plant at Betim (near Belo Horizonte) with the aid of large government subsidies. In sum, Minas manifests some branch-plant decentralization from São Paulo (dynamic B), some growth which is in fact part of the São Paulo economy (dynamic A), and some which is truly local in origin (traditional).

Paraná does not bear much discussion, notwithstanding its rapid rates of growth, since those come on top of a very small base, and the state's industrial economy remains very small. What can be observed and is of interest is the very high productivity in the state's dynamic A sector, and the resulting very high rate of worker exploitation, but the size of the sector is too small to make the example significant.

Santa Catarina presents a more interesting and complicated case. There was rapid growth across the board in this state in the 1970s. The traditional sector—which accounts for the lion's share of the state's industrial base—appears to be in the process of modernizing, as evidenced by its plant size, which is equal to that of São Paulo. Wages and productivity lag behind those in São Paulo but are higher than in most other states. The dynamic B sector appears to present an interesting story: it grew extremely rapidly, based on rather small plants (for this sector) with moderate wages but fairly high productivity. Modern products are apparently coming out of a very dynamic small plant sector in Santa Catarina: the characteristics of this ensemble appear to be unique to this state in Brazil (see chapter 8 for further discussion).

Table 4.6. Industrial structure and performance, Brazilian states.

	State[a]						Brazil
	SP	PR	RGS	MG	SC	RJ	
Employment, 1980 (%)							
Traditional	34.4	45.5	56.3	41.6	54.8	44.0	42.8
Dynamic A	30.5	33.2	23.6	37.9	27.3	28.7	30.3
Dynamic B	35.1	21.3	20.1	20.4	17.9	27.2	26.9
Change in output, 1970–80 (%)							
Traditional	46.2	103.5	104.9	62.0	138.7	14.2	60.8
Dynamic A	66.6	110.1	88.2	117.6	149.0	39.6	80.1
Dynamic B	114.5	350.1	196.7	262.2	223.4	78.3	137.8
Total industry	76.7	107.1	109.7	108.4	135.5	33.4	82.7
Plant size, 1980 (number of workers)							
Traditional	26.0	12.4	26.1	14.0	26.3	24.1	19.5
Dynamic A	36.3	16.0	18.8	16.8	22.3	35.4	20.6
Dynamic B	67.9	27.8	50.9	59.6	39.0	70.5	60.0
Total industry	37.3	15.4	27.3	18.0	25.6	33.0	24.3
Average wage, 1980 ($Cr h^{-1})							
Traditional	5.08	3.60	3.89	3.88	4.15	4.90	4.68
Dynamic A	7.89	4.68	5.41	6.54	4.28	7.01	7.00
Dynamic B	9.74	6.25	6.85	9.69	5.72	9.00	9.00
Total industry	7.57	4.52	4.84	6.08	4.46	6.62	6.62
Value added per worker, 1980 ($Cr)							
Traditional	28.6	27.4	22.2	21.7	26.3	28.8	24.9
Dynamic A	53.9	55.7	38.8	49.0	29.3	57.3	48.8
Dynamic B	40.5	23.9	28.9	34.6	35.9	40.1	38.3
Total industry	40.5	36.1	27.5	34.7	28.9	40.1	35.8
Output per worker, 1980 ($Cr)							
Traditional	73.3	87.4	54.3	63.9	68.7	68.6	64.0
Dynamic A	141.1	176.4	90.9	140.9	66.7	181.1	133.4
Dynamic B	89.1	51.4	53.1	65.9	75.5	71.7	88.0
Total industry	96.4	91.5	66.0	90.3	61.0	93.0	84.9
Value added per worker:wage per worker, 1980 (ratio)							
Traditional	5.63	7.61	5.71	5.59	6.33	5.87	5.32
Dynamic A	6.83	11.90	7.17	7.53	6.85	8.17	6.97
Dynamic B	4.16	3.83	4.21	3.57	6.28	4.46	4.14
Total industry	5.27	7.54	5.64	5.57	6.26	5.77	5.31

[a] See table 4.4.

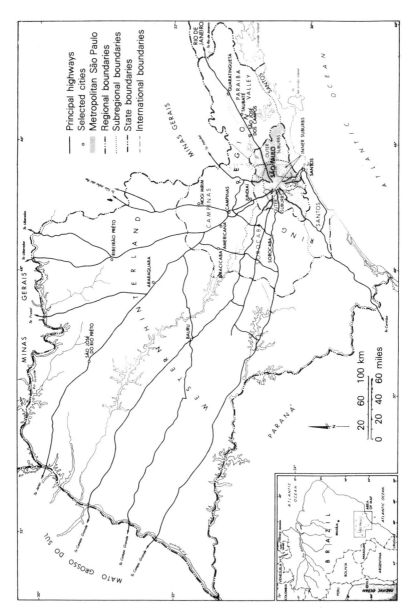

Figure 4.19. Regions of the state of São Paulo, showing southern part of Minas Gerais (source: International Bank for Reconstruction and Development).

Rio Grande do Sul has a rather large industrial base, where most of the growth in the 1970s was in the traditional and dynamic B ensembles. The traditional sector appears to be fairly modern, judging by its plant size, but it pays low wages and does not manifest very high levels of productivity— much lower, for example, than its neighbor Santa Catarina. One probable reason for this is that the product mix is different: there are more shoe factories (which require a higher labor input and are more difficult to industrialize) and less textiles than in Santa Catarina. The dynamic B sector, on the other hand, grew very rapidly, and appears to be a cross between São Paulo and Santa Catarina: plant size, wages, and productivity are all in the middle ranges, reflecting the fact that this sector is almost evenly divided between transportation equipment (trucks and cars) and machinery, unlike Santa Catarina where it is dominated by the machinery sector, or São Paulo and Minas, where transportation equipment is dominant. The transportation sector began to grow rapidly partly as a result of continuing integration of the Brazilian and Argentinian automobile industries; it is probable that some of the machinery sector grew in order to serve this primary demand.

Rio de Janeiro presents a series of paradoxes. All of its sectors have fairly large plants, high wages, high productivity, high output levels, and higher than average worker exploitation, yet the state's growth rates are persistently and dramatically below those of the rest of Southern and Southeastern Brazil. In other words, there is nothing in the numbers that suggests why investment should shun Rio, but that is in effect what continues to happen. The only plausible hypothesis, it would seem, is that Rio's proximity to São Paulo has become a positive disadvantage: there are few spatial market barriers between the two cities, and thus Rio can be served easily from São Paulo, which enjoys overwhelming external economies. In all the other areas (with the exception of the Sul de Minas, which is, as we have noted, really part of metropolitan São Paulo), there are important distance–cost barriers, which encourage the development of local industry. Why Rio is not favored as a branch-plant site, on the other hand, can probably be explained by the lack of land in Rio and the state's generally militant labor force, volatile political climate, and poorly organized and state-dependent capitalist class.

The evidence presented above hardly suggests the mechanisms of polarization reversal in the sense of a fundamental turning point in the pattern of geographical industrialization in Brazil. There is actually surprisingly little evidence of branch-plant decentralization from the state of São Paulo to other states. A few such plants, heavily aided by incentives, have indeed located outside of São Paulo, such as the aforementioned Fiat plant in Minas Gerais. But the great majority of branch or assembly plants are undertaking a very different kind of decentralization: they are locating in industrial towns within a 200-km radius of the city of São Paulo such as São José dos Campos, Piracicaba, Americana, Limeira, Rio Claro, and

Campinas (see figure 4.19). This extension of the 'agglomerative field' of São Paulo, that is, of the effective range of its agglomeration economies, actually has the effect of largely negating any advantages that might be had by locating such plants outside of the state of São Paulo, as has been demonstrated empirically in a recent study by Azzoni (1986). In other words, we are witnessing the extension of the localization economies of existing industrial complexes from a strictly 'urban' to a somewhat broader 'regional' scale.

There is surprisingly little evidence that locations in peripheral states present significant systematic economic advantages to producers. Certainly, wage rates—in absolute terms—do often remain below those of São Paulo, but so does productivity (table 4.7). Indeed, in those instances where we observed exploitation rates far above those of São Paulo (for example, dynamic A in Parana, Rio Grande do Sul, Minas, or Rio), we observed lower growth rates than in Santa Catarina, with a lower rate of exploitation. There is no straightforward relationship to be observed here. And, as we saw in the previous section, there is a tendency toward rapid interregional convergence of wage rates and thus exploitation rates for industries *with plants of similar sizes in Brazil.*

Why, then, would peripheral locations grow relatively more rapidly than São Paulo? The evidence does not lead to a definitive answer, but rather to some theoretically and empirically informed speculations. Some of the apparent locational dispersion may not be caused by dynamic growth processes, but may reflect precisely their opposite. The economic climate in Brazil has been extremely erratic since the mid-1970s, when the economic miracle began to run aground and when the statistical evidence on the reduction of São Paulo's relative dominance commences. It may be that during temporary upturns in production, small firms in outlying areas have entered production, precisely because they are flexible sources of production capacity. They are able to do so in part because they enjoy

Table 4.7. Indices of productivity, salaries, and surpluses, 1970, 1975, 1980 by sector, manufacturing industry (Brazil = 1.00) (source: Azzoni, 1986, page 64; *Censo Industrial* IBGE, 1970; 1980).

State[a]	Productivity			Salaries			Surpluses		
	1970	1975	1980	1970	1975	1980	1970	1975	1980
SP	1.12	1.08	1.05	1.11	1.12	1.05	1.12	1.07	1.05
RJ	1.11	1.02	1.01	1.08	0.97	0.95	1.11	1.03	1.02
MG	1.05	0.95	0.99	0.85	0.89	0.90	1.11	0.97	1.03
PR	1.03	1.09	1.09	0.88	0.90	0.86	1.08	1.14	1.14
SC	0.77	0.87	0.93	0.76	0.81	0.82	0.77	0.89	0.96
RS	0.88	0.88	0.87	0.86	0.87	0.87	0.88	0.88	0.87
Goais	1.06	0.90	1.03	0.80	0.77	0.76	1.13	0.92	1.08

[a] See table 4.4.

lower labor costs and fewer regulations than large firms and less scrutiny than they would face in São Paulo from labor unions and government. They are increasingly able to link into markets in São Paulo because of the massive investments in the road and communications systems which have been made in Brazil in recent times. The recent success of some local industrial complexes outside São Paulo, as evidenced in their growth rates, may precisely reflect their smaller scale and possibly more flexible divisions of labor than are present in São Paulo, where very large-scale industries—while highly productive—are also by definition easily hurt by economic fluctuations leading them to be reluctant to make large new investments in production capacity during the short upturns of the late 1970s and 1980s. The modernizing traditional ensembles of Rio Grande do Sul and Santa Catarina, and the special dynamic B ensemble of Santa Catarina are likely candidates here (Kipnis, 1983; personal communication, 1986).[13]

4.5 The 1980s: repolarization?
The 1980s have been a recessionary period in Brazil, in contrast to the previous decade. Total industrial employment actually fell from about 4.4 million to 3.7 million between 1980 and 1984, and in São Paulo the corresponding figures are 2.1 million and 1.75 million. The recession has dramatically interrupted the process of sectoral succession that appeared to be under way in the 1970s. As shown in table 4.2, traditional industries increased their share of employment and output at the expense of the dynamic A and B ensembles between 1980 and 1984. Meanwhile, São Paulo's shares of the dynamic A and B ensembles rose in the early 1980s, producing a slight increase in São Paulo's share of overall employment; *thus, the apparent tendency toward 'relative' polarization reversal observed in the 1970s came to a halt in the early 1980s.*

I argued earlier that for substantial reductions in São Paulo's absolute lead over peripheral states to come about, high levels of sustained growth would be required, thus propelling the processes of sectoral succession, increases in scale, and deepening of divisions of labor in the industrial economy. The very recent history of spatial industrial development in Brazil suggests that this is true also for the continuation of marginal shifts in shares of different places: any tendency toward this kind of limited decentralization is consequent upon growth, and to the extent that growth cannot be sustained, São Paulo's share will not diminish further.

The essential underlying weakness of the development process of peripheral areas is also underscored by the events of the 1980s. As the

---

[13] In late October and early November 1986, I visited the industries of Santa Catarina, and was guided through numerous factories and workshops in the textile and machinery industries there. Some of the firms visited include Irmaos Fischer, Buettner, Renaux, Artex, and Sulfabríl. I also spoke with individuals in government and community affairs in Blumenau and Joinvile.

traditional sector's share of the economy as a whole grew, São Paulo's share of that ensemble's employment dropped. In the 1980s, peripheral areas have gained in the traditional ensemble, while São Paulo has reasserted its dominance in the dynamic A and B ensembles (even as the share of those ensembles in the Brazilian economy as a whole dropped slightly). Peripheral areas, in other words, have shown that their strong point remains their specialization in traditional rather than modern goods.

4.6 Concluding observations

The information presented here is hardly ideal, for it does not permit us to penetrate the concrete details of industrial development in the different states. The evidence does, however, suggest a number of conclusions which can be summarized as follows.

First, even in a period of very active industrial growth—the 1970s—that growth was not sufficient to produce any evidence of a decline in São Paulo's real position; indeed, the absolute gaps between São Paulo and the rest of the country increased.

Second, trends toward what we might call 'relative decentralization', that is, shifts in shares, are tied very closely to growth, and, when growth ceases, so does growth of the periphery's share of employment or output. It seems that sustained growth, on the other hand, is closely related to sectoral succession in the industrial economy, which I have suggested would be necessary for long-term polarization reversal through repolarization.

Third, the explanatory power of both the neoclassical and the pure Kaldorian theories with respect to industrial location patterns seems to be rather limited. On the one hand, it does not appear that industries move automatically in response to the availability of cheaper factors of production. On the other hand, industries do not seem always to stay in place in the face of very high or increasing levels of worker exploitation (that is, the surplus of value added over wages). Moreover, there is an exceptionally rapid tendency for interstate wages to converge in Brazil, implying that the advantages to capitalists of spatial 'escape' are actually quite limited; this is probably not because wages are so 'high' in the peripheral areas, but because they have always remained quite 'low' in São Paulo, as we shall see in the following chapter. All in all, the economics of industrial location show few simple straightforward patterns, implying rather the existence of a field of constraints on and opportunities for locational change.

Fourth, and in line with the last point, the technological structure of industries varies from place to place, implying that different activities or forms of organization are employed in these different places. It seems also that changes in locational patterns in the course of growth are associated with changes in the technical structure of the industries at hand. We can guess that in the case of the outlying principal states of Brazil, this technological and organizational heterogeneity appears because many different processes were unfolding simultaneously in the 1970s: (a) location of modern assembly or branch plants outside of São Paulo; (b) modernization of traditional industries in the course of growth in output; and (c) 'endogenous' development of local, outlying industrial complexes in the modern industries, but using different techniques and organizational forms than are found in the same industries in São Paulo.

Fifth, none of these processes of spatial development, even when growth is quite strong, represents a weakening of São Paulo's agglomeration economies. Whether they could effect real polarization reversal would thus depend on the extent to which they could install their own self-generative agglomeration economies to the point that their growth would, in absolute terms, overtake that of São Paulo, *and* whether São Paulo will reach a point of severe agglomeration diseconomies and loss of growth, as has occurred in the industrial cores of some of the advanced capitalist countries.

In the following chapter, I will take up in detail two central questions which have been raised in this analysis. First, we need to know whether the Brazilian economy is capable of generating the kind of macroeconomic growth that could reignite the process of sectoral succession and deepening divisions of labor that are required for sustained growth of peripheral areas. Second, we need to know whether the São Paulo agglomeration has a tendency to generate diseconomies of agglomeration that might halt its growth and redirect greater absolute quantities of that growth elsewhere.

Macroeconomics and regional development:
why does polarization exist?

If any eventual possibility for dynamic, continuous polarization reversal is based on macroeconomic growth, then it is to the macroeconomy we must look in order to understand why many developing countries, even those with large industrial economies, exhibit continuing high levels of polarization in spite of efforts over several decades in some of them to reduce regional inequalities. Put in other terms, the question is whether currently developing countries necessarily must follow the paths as described in the five bell curves.

When we look over the growth pulses and the subsequent depressions in the last several decades in Brazil, the record is a mixed one. Industrial output has increased impressively in the last thirty years, but it has not advanced over its levels of the mid-1970s at this writing, and in many countries it is well below its 1979 peak (World Bank, 1984). Output levels are strongly dependent on export capability, a clear indication that these economies lack an internal propulsive dynamism, because import-substitution policies have saturated their potential internal markets. Income dynamics, too, present a mixed picture. It is doubtlessly true that per-capita income has increased in the last thirty years, in absolute terms. But distributions have tended to worsen (Bacha and Taylor, 1980). In some boom periods, absolute income levels appear to rise for the working class; but in Brazil, the urban working classes have lower average real incomes today than they had in the 1970s, even though the numbers of people with higher absolute incomes have increased (Bacha, 1978). A statistically valid rule of thumb for describing the Brazilian economy is that 30% of the population takes part in the consumption of significant quantities of modern industrial goods, while 70% does not, and these proportions have remained largely unchanged since the early 1970s (Fields, 1977). We could continue reviewing complex macroeconomic and social indicators, but the picture would remain the same: one without a clear sense that industrialization is 'deepening', even though it may be slowly 'widening' or growing in an absolute sense. In what follows, I describe the structure of this shallow type of industrialization, and identify its principal causes, suggesting why it is simultaneously *structurally* shallow and *temporally* sluggish, and that these are reasons why it remains *regionally dense*.

5.1 The problem of incomes and investment
The production-system analysis presented in the preceding chapters constitutes only one of the two great elements of a full understanding of economic dynamics from what can be variously called the Marxian, classical, or post-Keynesian perspectives. In this view, the fundamental circuit of the macroeconomy is composed of changes in productivity and

changes in income levels as well, the latter being responsible for the transformation (or lack thereof) of gains in productivity into investment, consumption, and expansion. Two initial points about the general nature of this relationship now need to be made.

First, in a modern capitalist economy, since production is founded upon dynamic returns to scale, an expansionist macroeconomic process may in the long run take care of its own supply limitations. This includes not only the supplies of labor and materials, but of all forms of capital, since there is always a tendency toward relative input saving in the system as a whole, even where capital–output ratios in certain specific branches of production may be rising (Kaldor, 1972; Sutcliffe, 1971). This is a relationship in general and in principle, of course; as we shall see, capitalist behavior is critical to its actualization. The point, though, is that the idea of a dynamic economy literally exhausting its capital supplies and requiring redistribution of income toward capitalists to support growth, is highly unlikely to occur, and only when the working class is both very rich and not saving at all.

Second, factor supply and productivity are in theory and in fact separable from the other side of the macroeconomy, which comprises factor demands, factor incomes, and aggregate demand. In neoclassical models, of course, the theory of productivity is simultaneously a theory of pricing and distribution. In a world of heterogeneous capital, on the other hand, there is no unique productivity–distribution relationship. This means that to analyze economic growth, it is inadequate to consider product markets and factor markets as somehow synchronized in general equilibrium. Factor markets—those of both capital and labor—have their own determinants, and their performance can be shaped by any number of complex technological, social, political, and institutional variables, and not simply by marginal productivity and the prices attached thereto.

Long-term capitalist growth requires a 'virtuous circle' between productivity, investment, and consumption. The problem is that investment and consumption (which depends on income) do not follow automatically from productivity, as Adam Smith and others seemed to think they would. Without them, the dynamic scale economies and Verdoorn effects which sustain dynamic expansion falter. The reasons for these separations between the two sides of the macroeconomy have preoccupied classical economists from Marx to Keynes; I shall advance an explanation which draws on both of these traditions.

The distribution of income is always contested in a capitalist society. Gains in productivity do not necessarily insure that there will be proportional changes in salaries. There is always a tension between the pursuit of individual gains (repression of workers' salaries and income share on the part of capitalists) and the optimal pattern of development of the system as a whole (distribution of a magnitude of income that would sustain auto-dynamic growth of the economy). Capitalist competition is the fundamental type of noncooperative game, in which the adversaries may impede the attainment of their own collective self-interest. This is especially the case in the developing countries.

Consider two ideal types of macroeconomy: one semi-industrialized and underdeveloped, the other industrialized and developed. In the first type, a high share of total income is concentrated in a fairly large middle class which is responsible for most of the consumption of durable goods. The great majority of the population, however, remains confined to the consumption of what is necessary for survival, and cannot acquire many durable goods. In this economy, complexes of modern industries develop, but the scale of their output tends to remain limited, and additional sectors are introduced into the economy only by the use of strong government policies for import substitution. The economy as a whole experiences short bursts of rapid growth followed by deep recessions. There are two reasons for this. First, the urban middle and upper classes cannot consume more than a certain quantity of durable goods. Yet it is only these latter products, by virtue of their technological qualities and thus their production processes, whose production is amenable to strong productivity gains. The low index of labor absorption in the most modern industrial sectors is insufficient to generate for the mass of population, levels of income that would permit their entry into many consumer markets. Second, the existence of an enormous surplus of labor-power impedes gains in average productivity, because it remains more expensive to substitute machines for labor in many activities. For example, in Brazil the middle class often continues to use domestic labor in place of machines for washing clothes. Thus, intersectoral relations and sectoral succession do not develop in a dynamic, self-propelling fashion. On the contrary, even though the economy supports a reasonably diversified industrial apparatus with many modern sectors, the average level of productivity in the economy remains low, and many backward sectors or phases of production continue to exist. The growth that does occur is primarily caused by the expansion of capitalist activity into new sectors or activities, usually by virtue of government policy (for example, commercialization of agriculture or introduction of innovative industrial sectors such as electronics). We can call this a market-*widening* strategy without market *deepening*; in Brazil, this takes the form of '30/70' society referred to earlier. This pattern can be described as a 'vicious circle', because each round of sectoral development exhausts its growth potential very rapidly.

As noted, it is frequently argued by conservative economists that the failure to realize growth in underdeveloped economies is caused by a shortage of capital (and thus, savings). The long-term problem is not a shortage of capital, however, but a failure to achieve productivity-raising investment with the wealth that is generated. Capitalists (or the wealthy in general) in these economies do not generally have confidence in the future of growth in commodity production—that is, in the types of goods and services subject to competition and efficiency increases. They therefore tend to restrict themselves to rent-earning activities or strictly oligopolizable production sectors.[14] In the latter, their investments are shielded from competition, and in the former, they are in general valorized by all the other speculators of their same social class. They also act as a class to insure that these kinds of capital gains are maintained and not taxed away. Although the personal incomes of the wealthy remain high, the incomes generated by the system remain much lower than they would be if investment were concentrated in competitive and technologically dynamic activities. The investors' 'animal spirits' are not right, as Keynes would have put it.

These dynamics with respect to income distribution, consumption, and investment reinforce each other. In all capitalist economies, there is a fundamental war over the division of the product into wages and profits. But in an underdeveloped economy, wage increases really are more difficult for the system to absorb in the short run because the intersectoral structure of production is less diverse and smaller in scale, and thus less capable of compensating wage changes with productivity changes. The capacity of the system to 'outrun' factor-supply problems is much more limited than in a developed economy, and this gives rise to the, mistaken, impression that growth is strangled by capital shortages. Wage increases are also a problem for capitalists in developed economies, but not always so much in this short-run sense; rather, in an economy with high levels of labor absorption, they rapidly create pattern effects and become a political-cum-economic problem over the medium run. In an underdeveloped economy, however, wage increases quickly upset the relative price system either because there is little unutilized capacity, or because oligopolistic market structures allow capitalists to pass their cost increases through to consumer prices. The different vicious circles reproduce each other.

The second type of macroeconomy centers on mass consumption, where a majority of the population consumes substantial quantities of modern goods. We might call this the '80/20' society of the United States or Western Europe. With rising real incomes, the real product wage is also rising, and may do so at a greater rate than real money income if productivity is rising rapidly enough. In any case, if the real product wage is rising, then aggregate elasticity of demand will increase. This is the *only* known way to sustain modern economic growth. Even if product prices are reduced through increasing productivity, product-demand elasticities are normally insufficient—taken alone—to compensate for job losses associated with the technologies that increase productivity. Incomes must rise in real money and real product terms (Sen, 1963).

[14] I might add that the oligopolistic structure of the industrial economy also lies behind the inflationary tendencies of economies such as that of Brazil. With little price competition, costs are simply passed through, maintaining a constant distributional structure in the economy as a whole.

This process of productivity and income growth spurs the process of a sectoral succession in the economy as a whole, that is, leads to the development of new production sectors. There exists a large quantity of income in the economy, distributed among a large number of consumers (whether individuals or enterprises) capable of supporting the initial development and production of new types of goods and processes. From time to time, new groups of industries—whether in the form of new final demand sectors or new types of capital goods—arise and change the sectoral locus of capitalist growth.[15]

Sectoral succession makes two critical, interconnected contributions to macroeconomic growth. First, new product sectors are not technologically mature, and so they do not have routinized, vertically integrated production processses. There tends to be less price competition initially than when technologies and production methods are well diffused in the economy. As a result, they often generate superprofits (rents). For the same reason, employment – output ratios are higher in new industries than in older ones, and there is a relatively high proportion of skilled labor. Moreover, high levels of product change and innovation in processes generate a great deal of new employment.

As a result, the economy as a whole transfers employment from older sectors with low employment-output ratios to new sectors; compensates for the stagnation of older markets by the creation of new ones; and provides opportunities for superprofit in the face of high levels of competition and lowered profits in older sectors which are no longer oligopolistic (see Markusen, 1985). This is the phenomenon known as the 'super-multiplier'. All this occurs even while *average* (intersectoral) productivity continues to increase. The economy is founded upon deepening of markets through this 'virtuous circle' of employment, distribution, innovation, and productivity.[16]

[15] There is much dispute over whether these sectors evolve according to regular patterns, as was argued by Kondratieff in his notion of long waves of capitalist growth. Here, we need not enter this particular debate, noting simply that in dynamic economies there is a tendency to extend the intersectoral division of labor over time through the development of new groups of industrial ensembles.

[16] This is an idealized picture of shifting regimes of accumulation in capitalist economies, of course. Transitions between industrial ensembles are likely to be very difficult processes, involving all manner of social and political struggles and resulting in different macrosocial and political arrangements as well as new forms of production. Moreover, there is nothing necessarily permanent about each regime of accumulation, in the sense that in a capitalist economy it is likely that each regime of accumulation will at some point reach its limits and fall into crisis. At the same time, it must be noted that transitions within economies based on articulated and intensive accumulation in the last 100 years have not simply involved the replacement of one dominant locus of accumulation by another with the level of economic development remaining the same throughout. Instead,

The consequences of each of these different types of macroeconomy for the development of regions in the respective countries should already be apparent. In the macroeconomic model that describes the economies of semi-industrialized countries such as Brazil and Mexico, extensive accumulation is linked to a very high level of interregional polarization of economic activity and population, that is, to very high levels of interregional inequalities. In the intensive macroeconomic model, in which we include the USA, Canada, and West Germany, autodynamic accumulation has historically been associated with relatively low levels of polarization and interregional inequalities. This latter type of macroeconomy can increase its number of sectors and quantity of output in a dynamic fashion, through the continuous deepening of markets. A multiplicity of regional production complexes develops because each new dominant ensemble enjoys a window of locational opportunity. Each ensemble tends to generate endogenously its own external economies of scale at its preferred locations. Increases in the scale of production of older industries also make it possible for them to reorganize and shift out of their old centers into new industrial peripheries. The process of regional industrial development, like the process of industrialization, is dynamic; it contains strong inherent pressures to depolarize the economy through the creation of new growth centers and new growth peripheries.

On the basis of the analysis presented above, it can be seen that polarization reversal is not an historical necessity, for it rests on a form of macroeconomic development which itself is not an automatic outcome of the industrialization process. A distribution of income capable of sustaining dynamic accumulation and sectoral succession is not the necessary correlate of industrialization or productivity development. It is here that the limits of any production-system analysis are confronted. The process of growth of any capitalist economy depends on its social relations; there is no such thing as growth that flows 'naturally' or inevitably from technology or from the division of labor in production.

(16) (continued)
subsequent regimes of accumulation have tended to absorb labor displaced by innovations through growth, and to build intersectoral relations in a progressive fashion. Thus, rather than simple failure of one mode of extensive or extractive accumulation and its replacement by another—as in many Third World economies— we find a highly articulated set of intersectoral relations, progressive growth of incomes, and so on. This is roughly faithful to the development of US capitalism during the last century, and has been successfully duplicated by the *dirigiste* state in France, the corporatists in Germany and, for a time, the labor–capital standoff in Britain.

5.2 Migration, urban labor markets, and polarization

The critical factor market which influences the distributional conditions described above is, of course, the labor market. It is only in light of the structure of urban labor markets that the persistence of a demand structure which restricts dynamic growth in the underdeveloped economies can be understood. Since the argument to be made about labor markets and wage determination will be complex, it will perhaps be helpful to preview the main conclusions that will be reached. Rural–urban population movements create urban labor surpluses in large Third World industrial cities, in the form of high rates of urban unemployment. These surpluses are both result of and cause of wage-setting processes. The wage levels that result contribute to spatial polarization in two ways: first, they directly reduce the development of agglomeration diseconomies in the large centers of industrial production; second, they are one of the main reasons why the distribution of income remains so unequal, thus contributing to the 'Smithian' polarization described in the previous section. The policy conclusion is also very clear: to change processes of *urban* wage determination, the supply elasticity of rural population to the urban centers at existing prices must be reduced. The only other conceivable way to change the distribution of income would be to wait for labor-absorbing growth to occur; but, as I have already described, this is precisely what is unlikely to occur without changes in the structure and quantity of product demand in the economy, which itself requires changes in the structure of income. Let me now elaborate this argument in some detail.

There is an enormous literature on the problems of labor absorption, labor markets, and wage determination in the Third World. I do not pretend to review it here, but instead to draw on it for points of reference. The early treatments of the subject date from Lewis (1954) and Kuznets (1955) (later developed in a more modern version by Fei and Ranis, 1964). The Lewis two-sector model became the received 'general theory' of development processes in labor-surplus countries. Lewis was interested in the generation of a reserve army of labor and its absorption during the growth process. His basic idea is that the economy consists of a traditional, rural subsistence sector characterized by low productivity and therefore 'surplus' labor, and a modern urban industrial sector with high productivity. Labor is transferred from the rural to the urban sector as output expands in the latter. The speed of transfer is given by the rate of output expansion, which in turn is a function of the accumulation of capital. Urban capitalists accumulate insofar as they earn profits, and it is assumed that they reinvest all these profits to expand output. The level of urban wages is initially set exogenously by some increment over rural subsistence. At this urban wage, there is a perfectly elastic supply of urban labor until the rural–urban transition is effected; then, labor is absorbed and wage-determination dynamics must shift into the pattern which is characteristic of a developed country.

Kuznets (1955) invented a companion theory of income distribution in the course of development, whose temporal pattern he described as an 'inverted U curve', (this is one of the 'five bell shapes' referred to in section 1.1). Income inequality first rises as industrialization is initiated, because the urban sector has wide skill differentials as compared with the rural sector. Short-run skill inelasticities develop. However, as output expands and with it the urban labor force, these economy-wide skill inelasticities diminish, in turn reducing income inequality. As more workers are absorbed into the urban sector, supply and demand at different skill levels become equilibrated and the low-skill rural sector is reduced in size. Hence, the income distribution passes the inflection point of the curve and becomes more equal.

There are serious problems with the way these models conceptualize labor demand and the behavior of labor supplies, which give clues as to why the improvements in income distribution they envision have not materialized in many of the developing countries. Most of the fundamentals of factor demand have already been discussed in our previous treatments of technology, but they can be recalled briefly here. The basic quantity of factors demanded per unit of output is more a function of the scale of production (technology) than anything else. At any given scale, factor proportions are relatively inflexible. Lewis does not go as far as a pure neoclassical approach, which hinges on substitutions governed by price elasticities, but he does assume that factor proportions remain the same as output increases and capitalists add labor until its marginal physical product is equated to price. The problem, of course, is that, as output rises, labor usage tends to drop because of scale economies, so Lewis's labor-absorption assumptions, like those of the pure neoclassicals, are inconsistent with the reality of Third World industry. The second problem is that capitalists do not necessarily reinvest their profits to expand output; they often simply reinvest in rentier activities (see previous section). Thus, even when the capital supply increases, there is no necessity for output, and thus labor absorption, to increase.

There is historically only one basic way to escape these traps and establish the kind of growth experienced by the developed economies, as I pointed out in the previous section: to raise real wages (in terms of a bundle of products, that is, the 'real product wage' and not simply the real money wage), so that the *elasticity* of demand increases along with capital accumulation and increasing returns to scale. Without this type of increase, product-demand elasticities are usually insufficient—even when increased efficiencies are passed through in lower prices, as they are in most Third World economies, and not kept as profit gains—to support the growth required to effect the transition to full employment in the modern urban sector.

This brings us to the labor-market dynamics that impede such a rise in the real product wage. We may start with the realistic assumption that real money wages in urban labor markets are 'sticky downward'. They do not fall in response to rising unemployment. They sometimes fall in countries like Brazil when wages are deindexed from inflation. On average, however, real money wages are set institutionally and tend to be stabilized this way. Wages are already so low that it requires major political force (such as a military coup) to reduce them, even if unemployment is high.

Under these conditions, the dynamics described by the well-known Todaro–Harris (TH) migration model come into being. The TH model postulates that rural to urban migration proceeds in response to urban–rural differences in *expected* rather than actual earnings. Migrants consider the various opportunities available to them in the rural and urban sectors, and they attempt to maximize their 'expected' income. These expected gains are measured by the difference in real incomes between rural and urban work opportunities and the probability that a new migrant will secure an urban job.

Migrants, of course, understand that there is high underemployment and unemployment in the cities of their countries. Why, then, do they keep migrating? If there are significant urban–rural wage differentials, and there is a reasonable probability of gaining one of these jobs, then the migrant's expected income in the city will be higher than in the rural area. For example, if the wage in a rural area in Brazil is Cr\$ 800 per month, while in an urban area jobs begin at Cr\$ 2000 per month, and the worker has a 60% probability of getting one of these jobs within a year, then his or her expected urban income is Cr\$ 1200 per month. This assumes only a one-period time horizon. If we take the realistic case where the vast majority of migrants are between 15 and 24 years old, and thus looking toward a lifetime of income, the probabilities are very high indeed that income increases will be had by migrating. In our example of wage differentials, it would be necessary to have an urban unemployment rate of 60% to vitiate the private profitability of further migration. Thus, even with the sizable rates of urban unemployment (that is, sometimes 30–40%) in many cities, it is not surprising that migration continues. It seems to approach zero only in very severe depressions, as in the early 1980s in Brazil.

Aggregate rates of unemployment may even underestimate the probability that a given individual will obtain a job. As noted earlier (section 2.2), as the absolute size of the urban labor market grows, the greater is its level of turnover. This is caused, in general, by the greater level of vertical disintegration and the more elaborate social division of labor in industrial activities in large cities, as compared with other places. Because of this, the probability that any individual will find work is greater, the larger the absolute size of the labor market. Jayet (1983) has formalized these relationships with the observation that workers in urban areas tend to experience more frequent alternations of employment and unemployment, whereas workers in nonurban areas tend to experience more prolonged bouts of unemployment once they lose their jobs (see also Scott and Storper, 1987; Sirmans, 1977; Stiglitz, 1974; Vipond, 1974).

In consequence of all these factors, it remains rational for people to migrate to the city, even if wages are, in absolute terms, not very high. As such, the supply of labor grows in the cities and it is not counteracted by dropping wages. At the same time, stable or decreasing employment– output ratios in many industries assure that migration will result in a structural labor surplus. This migration process contributes to urban population increases and a tendency for industrial centers to become very large in terms of population as well as primate in terms of economic activity.

Now we can trace the effects of this labor-supply situation on wage determination and income distribution. The first thing to note is that urban labor markets are segmented: the wage-determination dynamics for skilled and professional jobs are different from those for the average unskilled job. The evidence for this is revealed in research on income inequality. Had the relative wages of all occupations changed in propor- tion to their supply–demand profiles in the 1960s and 1970s in Brazil, the skilled occupations would have had decreases, because their supplies increased much more rapidly relative to demand then did unskilled supplies (Bacha, 1978; Bacha and Taylor, 1980). In reality just the opposite occurred. Increasing income inequality in the Brazilian economy was partly the result of a widening wage spread, with the skilled workers gaining much more than the unskilled workers.[17] We must therefore assume that the labor markets for these different types of jobs are segmented: they have different wage-determination processes.

The question is how the rural–urban migration process affects wage determination in the unskilled sector—that is, the majority of manufactur- ing jobs—so as to make the wage spread possible. One explanation is, of course, that various authoritarian governments have used 'wage-squeeze' policies to repress wages. But this explanation is at best partial, since there have been periods when these governments explicitly relaxed their wage-repression policies, and throughout much of the 1970s in Brazil legislation actually protected real money wage minima. Nonetheless, wages for unskilled workers in modern urban industries have still failed to rise as much in real terms as productivity in those same industries.

---

[17] There were actually two sources of increasing income inequality: the wage spread alluded to here and increasing inequality in the functional income distribu- tion (that is, between wages and profits, as well as between wage levels). That is, the rich kept getting richer as a consequence of wealth accumulation which generates profits and rents for them. These are in addition to the increasing discrepancies of wage income as reflected in the wage spread. Moreover, much of the real discrepancy of income is probably unreported, since so much nonwage income is unmeasured in countries such as Brazil.

In the unskilled segment, it would appear that rural–urban migration is critical to urban wage determination for two reasons. First is that rural populations and the urban unemployed represent an enormous reserve army of labor that can be tapped by employers without having to make great wage concessions. The elasticity of urban labor supplies depends only on *some* difference with rural wages combined with a certain probability that a worker will obtain a job. Salaries thus remain very low relative to productivity gains. There is nothing short of rural wage increases that could reduce the elasticity of urban labor supplies, in this logic. The result is that labor-supply elasticities are very high, even though labor-demand elasticities are relatively low in modern capital-intensive industries.

Second, the political dimensions of wage determination for urban unskilled workers are influenced by labor-supply elasticity. In the first place, the naturally occurring high turnover characteristic of urban labor markets, combined with the aggregate surplus, allows producers to use deliberate labor-turnover policies as a means of reducing militancy and curbing labor's incipient bargaining power (Humphrey, 1982). Turnover ceases to be related uniquely to cycles of labor demand, but comes to be a key *social relation* in the labor market as well. In addition, migrants tend to be politically self-selecting. They go to the city with economic goals, and they are notoriously reluctant to sully their political reputations with employers if they feel that long-term economic gains remain possible for them. Migrants are often what sociologists call urban 'peasant workers' in terms of their political behavior; they have one foot in the countryside in that they are not politically experienced as members of an *urban* working class (Sabel, 1982). Employers play on these attitudes by selectively using turnover to discipline the most militant members of the work force, while setting up elaborate wage hierarchies within the larger plants which are then used to hold out the—rarely realized—prospect of advancement (Humphrey, 1982). The hierarchies thus reinforce the fierce individualism of many of the peasant workers.

The end result is that, even though urban wages are usually greater than rural income, they remain in general quite low relative to productivity and they tend to stagnate in real product terms. They impede increases in the consumption power of the working class, such as would be required to induce a different course of macroeconomic growth. Urban salaries do not develop the same levels of diseconomies that eventually develop in many other urban factor markets, such as those for transportation and land.[18]

---

[18] There is an irony in the spatial wage patterns described here. In developed economies with many industrial cities (and where wages are not set by national unions or the state), wages in regions of rapid growth will tend to grow faster than the national average. In spite of the high levels of spatial integration of the national economy, divergent growth rates between places and sectoral diversity bring

The retardation of wage gains contributes to polarization in two ways. First, agglomeration diseconomies that might be expected to accompany growth are reduced. This discourages the outward movement of existing industries. Second, wage levels make an important indirect contribution to polarization, for restriction of consumption power limits the extent of the market and so reproduces the 'Smithian' dynamic of polarization, consisting of limited scale in existing industries and a tendency to stagnation in the overall sectoral composition of the industrial economy, thus inhibiting sectoral succession and the creation of new territorial growth centers.[19]

5.3 Getting beyond the theme of imperialism
The theme of imperialism has been central to much scholarly analysis of Third World development in general and regional economic development in particular over the past several decades, and this includes the analysis of polarization and overurbanization. It has assumed various guises, including those of world systems analysis and dependency theory, a concern with the transnational corporation, and many varieties of theory centering on the role of trade in national and regional development.

[18] (continued)
considerable interregional wage differences. In underdeveloped economies with *lower* levels of spatial integration, there is one basic spatial wage disparity: between rural areas and their service centers, and large cities or urbanized regions. Among urbanized regions, industrial wage levels then tend to be quite similar, in spite of dramatic variations in productivity, sectoral composition, and rate of growth. The aggregate labor-market conditions do not exist to make the differences found in developed economies come about.

Note that I am making assumptions very similar to the Kaldor model when it comes to productivity, but not when it comes to spatial wage patterns. In the end, however, Kaldor's basic point would hold, that is, that the differences between productivity levels and nominal wages would determine efficiency salaries and indicate the presence or absence of Verdoorn effects (Kaldor, 1970). For a more detailed discussion, and evidence for the Brazilian case, see chapter 4.

[19] One additional specific aspect of continued polarization should be highlighted. We noted that labor supplies are created endogenously as industrial complexes form themselves and proliferate their social division of labor. In some senses, this presents little problem in highly developed economies such as the United States, where the majority of the labor force is accustomed to work in the formal economy under its conditions of regulated wage labor. In the Third World economies, however, it is easy to discover areas where much of the population has not had contact with the formal sector, or where their experience of waged work has been sporadic. Polarization thus feeds on itself, for when little industrialization outside of the central pole of the country is taking place, suitable labor supplies are not formed in peripheral cities and regions, reinforcing the risks and difficulties for new industries or plants to locate in these places. This process of endogenous labor-market creation, which is the creation of skills, work norms, and habituation to waged work, obviously is more complex in an underdeveloped economy. For this reason, the growth impulses that motivate the creation of new industrial complexes must be quite strong and sustained over time.

The argument presented in this chapter implies, in contrast to all these perspectives, that the role of imperial forces in producing the many failures of industrialization and regional development policy in the Third World in the 1960s and 1970s has frequently been exaggerated. In the process, scholars have frequently forfeited careful analysis of the diversity of local responses to global forces, and especially the roles of domestic class relations, politics, and policies in the developing countries and regions themselves in producing the wide differences observed in developmental outcomes. We can see this by reflecting very briefly on the recent history of industrialization and regional development strategies in countries such as Brazil.

From the 1950s through the 1970s in the larger Latin American countries such as Brazil and Mexico, industrial modernization was widely undertaken via the policy of import substitution. It was expected that forced diversification of the industrial apparatuses of these countries would hasten the advent of self-sustaining development. There was widespread ideological convergence about the merit of these policies, but for different reasons. The right typically endorsed modernization programs so long as the multinational corporations were let in to do the job; the left concurred, because import substitution had a strong affinity to Trotsky's theory of 'combined and uneven development' which in turn strongly embodied the productionist bias of much traditional Marxist development theory. Both of these groups, moreover, converged in their support of local content requirements, thus affirming their nationalist sentiments for economic independence (de Oliveira, 1977).

In many respects, the successes of such policies were impressive. In countries such as Brazil, in a period of just a few decades, the increases in industrial production, in the diversity of the industrial economy, in the sophistication of what is made and in the range of products manufactured, and in the levels of national income, were spectacular until the 1980s. The 1980s, however, are virtually a 'lost decade' in terms of such quantitative increases in the level of development. Moreover, throughout the process the developmental trajectory was marked by grotesque social and economic distortions: relative and absolute impoverishment of large segments of the population; rapid rural-to-urban migration and creation of the 'dangerous classes' in the cities; vicious macroeconomic cycles of boom, hyperinflation, and stagflation; increasing indebtedness; bloated bureaucracies; and pharaonic infrastructural and industrial undertakings with borrowed funds while basic needs of the population remained unmet. For these and other reasons, the model of industrialization fell into disrepair by the early 1980s.

Throughout, the right has blamed the failures of the model on the policy interventions themselves and endorsed freer markets (for the most part)—this includes both the national right and the international lending institutions. The left assigns blame to the transnational corporations who, they claim, are profit-takers who refuse to reinvest in countries in which they produce, and who exploit Third World workers in order to lower costs and raise profits at home. The two sides converged again in the 1980s, however, around a nationalistic response to the debt question, arguing that interest payments inhibit investment at home and reproduce dependency by transferring economic surplus abroad. Factions of the various national bourgeoisies (especially in Brazil) also agree with the left on the merits of market protections for such industries as high technology (for example, the Brazilian *lei de informática*).

A third response, which is neither exactly right-wing nor left-wing, centers on the forces of production themselves. I refer to the appropriate-technology theorists, who argue that the failures of large-scale modernization are as Lewis (1954) captured them in his labor-surplus analysis: unlike Lewis, however, they attribute the surplus almost entirely to the use of imported technologies and they conclude that such technologies deserve rejection in favor of those that are much more labor intensive (see chapter 6 for a more detailed discussion of appropriate technology theories).

All three of these positions thus share a focus on the role of external forces in the development of underdevelopment, whether it be technological biases, profit repatriation, the international trade system, or the workings of the international capital investment and finance organizations.

5.3.1 What went wrong: a counterpoint

As we have seen in this chapter, a missing ingredient in any valid explanation for why these countries never entered into a phase of balanced macroeconomic growth and expansion is that they never raised wages to the point where higher incomes could permit expansion of consumption on the part of the population at a rate sufficient to support continued, steady industrial investment. What resulted was a classic 'Keynesian' trap: highly productive industries were inserted into economies lacking the income growth to support continued expansion of consumption of their products.

Why did this happen? There are many competing interpretations. Causality can be assigned to technology itself, where the argument holds that limited labor-absorption capacity leaves huge surpluses of labor, who can then be exploited readily; hence, wages and consumption power remain perpetually restricted. There are a number of logical correlates to this view, however. For one, it was mostly the policies of the industrializing countries themselves that insisted on bringing these technologies in through the import-substitution process. This was their method of 'combining' and thus 'skipping over' the 'natural' stages of development. Second, some countries have successfully adapted imported technologies to local markets and factor-supply conditions, whereas others have not: the former category is exemplified by the Japanese automobile industry in the early postwar period, whereas Brazil and Mexico fall into the latter category (Cusumano, 1985). In other words, technological adaptation is not impossible, but it depends on local agents; to do this in Latin America would, to be sure, have required limiting or more closely guiding the participation of the transnationals in the import-substitution process, but this strategy was not pursued by countries such as Brazil in the 1950s (Evans, 1987). We therefore do not know whether they could have succeeded in getting the transnationals to use a different technology mix. Third, technology is not a deus ex machina: it takes social agents, in this case employers, to take advantage of the loose labor markets generated by capital-intensive industries. In Brazil the real culprits in this regard are not the employers in the large factories directly owned by the transnational corporations (who generally pay the highest wages in the industrial sector, although still very low by developed country standards), but the domestically owned enterprises, many of which are backwardly and forwardly linked to the transnationals (Macedo, 1980; Vieira da Cunha and Bonelli, 1978). These firms have typically exploited labor surpluses to a far greater extent than their multinational partners and only rarely have significant policies to prevent such exploitation by protecting labor been implemented (Argentina under Perón and Chile between 1968 and 1973 being the notable exceptions). Fourth, and closely related to the latter point, the national bourgeoisies, and their confreres in the military in such countries as Brazil, Argentina, and Chile, have been largely responsible for the brutal repression of the labor movements that might have successfully pressed for higher wages. Indeed, national industrial bourgeoisies and military interests in Brazil have never fully broken with the rural landed elites, and the latter often pursue interests inimical to the development of a full-fledged modern industrial–urban economy. In Brazil, for example, there is a tacit pact between industrial and rural elites to avoid land reform, which is, arguably, what would be necessary to stem the flow of labor to the cities and thus break the circle of low urban wages and consequent industrial underdevelopment. Both the urban–industrial and the rural elites profit by reinvesting their superprofits in rent-earning activities (such as real estate speculation) and urban–industrial elites would undoubtedly be threatened by a more truly competitive and less oligopolistic economy. Put in this light, the social agents who have actively impeded the realization of the income–consumption circuit which would have been necessary for an expansionist industrialization process associated with import substitution are hardly exclusively external to these countries, nor can their actions be seen as having been dictated by the abstract needs of international capitalism in the 1950s, 1960s, and 1970s.

   To be sure, some analyses, most especially that of Evans (1979), have stressed the joint roles of multinational, state, and local capital in developmental processes. There is considerable force behind the notion that the interests of Third World 'developmentalist' states and external capitals have converged substantially at times. For example, the strategy of import substitution was an extremely logical undertaking in the 1950s and 1960s both for domestic and for foreign interests. The dominant regime of industrialization in the advanced economies, Fordist mass production, was technologically of a nature such that it could, in large part, be picked up and implanted in new locations with little loss in efficiency, provided that a certain minimal scale of operations was met. This is because products and processes had both entered a phase of relatively high standardization and stability; dynamic economies of learning had levelled off and had been built into the machinery itself in many sectors. The transnational corporations and the richer national economies were also in good positions to transfer resources abroad: they enjoyed high profits, a stable international monetary system, and relatively little foreign trade competition (especially the United States). The latter point signifies that many of their investments in places such as Brazil were designed to serve local markets and not simply—as it is often mistakenly held—to use foreign locations in order to reduce costs of goods reimported to the North.[20] International conditions, then, were extremely propitious to the success of import-substitution policies. In spite of this logic of convergent interests, however, actual behavior was frequently otherwise: the domestic political and social conditions necessary to unleash a virtuous cycle of rising wages and consumption were never allowed to flourish by domestic capital or the state in much of the Third World. There is every reason to think, moreover, that rational multinational corporations would have preferred greater Third World growth, for this would have enlarged their markets, notwithstanding the higher wages they would have been obliged to pay labor in their Third World factories.

It should be clear by now that we can locate some of the failures of the development model in Brazil over the last few decades at least in part in the shape of domestic politics and class relations there, and it is a fair guess that this lesson applies to the other industrializing Third World countries themselves (and by the same token, developmental successes must at least in part then be credited to domestic forces). This is what has recently been labelled a 'postimperialist' perspective, denoting a re-emphasis on the complexity, diversity, and importance of local (that is, in the developing nations themselves) social relations in shaping the outcomes of their interactions with transnational forces (Becker and Sklar, 1987; Corbridge, 1988). In this regard, I am echoing a point which can be traced back at least as far as Cardoso (1977), who warned us to beware of investing historical outcomes with too much retrospective inevitability. This is

---

[20] The relocation of production to the Third World to cut costs (by reimporting finished goods) was not a particularly important strategy for the transnational manufacturing firms until the late 1970s, and still accounts for only a tiny fraction of the industrial production of the advanced countries; what has grown most rapidly over the last ten years is competition of imports of the advanced countries to each other (Gordon, 1988).

nowhere more emphatically needed than in the analysis of development processes apparently heavily affected by transnational corporations or a putative 'global capitalism' (Lipietz, 1986).

Just as it is necessary to get beyond analyses of the development failures of the 1960s and 1970s which ignore domestic class relations and political forces in favor of an all-encompassing focus on the forces of imperialism, so is the same true of the analysis of urbanization and regional development. We have already observed in this chapter that the wage levels typical of *Paulistana* industry are not sufficiently higher than the rest of the country in many cases even to compensate for cost of living differences, much less to give labor a constant share of output. People keep migrating to São Paulo because of a series of 'push' factors, and these are principally in the countryside: massive and often brutal agricultural modernization processes that have displaced literally millions of people from the land, such that huge areas remain at very low levels of productivity while others continue to be marked by the high levels of landownership concentration typical of *latifúndia*. These push processes have complex origins within Brazilian society itself. We may cite just a few such origins: (a) the *coronéis* (traditional landed elites) of the Brazilian Northeast have been a powerful political and social bloc within the Brazilian social formation for centuries, and their existence has little to do with modern industrial capitalism (Holanda, 1936); (b) the persistent failure of any meaningful land reform in Brazil (which might allow greater numbers of people to remain on the land, as it once did in Korea), which is essentially caused by the political blockages at the national level created by alliances between rural elites, the military, and an insufficiently mobilized, inattentive, and, at times, complicit urban – industrial bourgeoisie; (c) the wide support for nationalistic geopolitical ideologies of regional occupation in the Amazon, and the ideological reverence promoted with respect to modern agricultural technologies at many levels of the state and society (Hecht and Cockburn, 1989). Although multinational corporations sell chemicals and equipment to modernized farms, there is little evidence that they exercise any significant direct influence on the formation of Brazil's rural development policies. International lending institutions and agricultural technicians from developed countries certainly cooperate in fostering the processes that push people off the land, but the evidence suggests that they are but junior partners to Brazilian development authorities (Hecht, 1986).

Turning to attempts to reduce the 'pull' of population to the largest cities through decentralization of production, it is evident that the transnationals have been generally ahead of their national counterparts. The factories of multinational firms, for example, have the strongest presence in such places well outside of São Paulo as São José dos Campos, or the ring of cities such as Americana, Rio Claro, Limeira, Piracicaba, and so on, or—to take a more dramatic example—Fiat in Betím in the state of

Minas Gerais. This can be easily accounted for by virtue of the generally large scale of the plants of the transnationals, their highly standardized production processes and hence low unit costs of transporting inputs and outputs, their relatively stable labor requirements and hence their lesser need to be near a large, flexible pool of labor than smaller firms. It is evident that, were sufficient infrastructural supports available, transnationals would be happy to locate their plants well outside the traditional core areas of the country because of their long-distance linkage capabilities and because this would enable them to pay even lower wages than they do in São Paulo and to escape the relatively militant unions found there (Storper, 1984).

Where macroeconomic expansion is stunted by the low income trap for the working class described earlier, however, the dynamic of sectoral succession is likely to be severely retarded. The failure to attain greater regional dispersion of industrial development is, then, traceable directly to the internal limitations of the development model itself, and this development model is at least equally rooted in domestic forces as it is in the structure of the world economy.

Polarization and less developed regions:
a critique of assumptions

The analysis of the interrelations of polarization, technical change, and macroeconomic dynamics presented in previous chapters permits us now to evaluate critically some received ideas about polarization. The ideas to be examined here are important because they are the assumptions behind many regional policies in industrializing Third World countries. First, we examine the notion that polarization within the process of industrialization is largely avoidable (section 6.1). Then, we look at claims that polarized industrial regions are directly responsible for the underdevelopment of regional peripheries in industrializing countries (section 6.2). Finally, we assess the logic and method of attempts to even out regional development by redistributing activities away from polarized regions, especially in the form of urban–industrial growth-pole policies (section 6.3). These criticisms will form the basis for a set of positive recommendations for regional policy in the final chapters of this book.

6.1 Technology, the division of labor, and the geographical form of industrialization

In chapters 2 and 3 we argued that industrialization typically takes a polarized geographical form in its early stages because of the way the division of labor develops. There are critical assumptions about technology in that argument which now need to be made explicit as a prelude to considering whether there are alternative organizational and geographical possibilities in the course of modern industrialization.

Perhaps the technological assumptions which lie behind this argument can be best understood if they are set in the context of competing visions. It has been forcefully argued that there are alternative forms of production organization to those which have dominated industrialization in countries such as Brazil and Mexico, and that such alternatives are superior in terms of overall developmental effects. Some of these have also been proposed explicitly for their alleged ability to reduce spatial polarization. These alternatives take two major forms, both of which fundamentally de-emphasize the role of external economies of scale.

The first such strategy is the famous 'big push' model of development, in which an economy is forced to develop, very rapidly, the full inter-sectoral complement of the productive forces, at a relatively large scale of operation (Rostow, 1961). This initial push is supposed to lead to a takeoff, which then becomes self-sustaining. Even though this has not actually occurred in any developing country, it continues to generate intellectual fascination. This 'hyperproductivity' strategy is based on very different asumptions about production scale, the division of labor, and spatial behavior than were outlined in chapters 2 and 3. In principle, many industries would simply skip over the stage of vertical disintegration, going directly to higher levels of scale and thus developing very large internal scale economies and routinized external linkages. A lower level of spatial polarization would thus become possible.

The logic of the big push is exactly the opposite of the 'unbalanced growth strategy' offered by Hirschman (1955) and Perroux (1958), in which selective sectoral modernization would gradually force the modernization of other sectors. To make the big push work, an economy would have to be capable of creating, very suddenly, markets sufficiently large to absorb the output of a production system organized around massive internal returns to scale. Even the major Third World exporters have not been able to do this.

The second alternative de-emphasizes economies of scale altogether, arguing that industrialization should proceed via the adoption of 'appropriate' technologies in the modern sectors, while diminishing the aggregate importance of these sectors in the early stages of industrialization in favor of the more traditional industries. These latter industries should then also be developed using intermediate technologies. Thus, the strategy involves changes in techniques as well as changes in the sectoral composition of development. The basic idea is that this strategy would simultaneously minimize the social as well as the spatial dislocations associated with industrialization.

Although this represents a pleasant vision of economic development, its feasibility is open to question. First, what is the practical range of technological (and hence, organizational) choice faced by Third World countries in the development of modern industry? It conforms neither to the caricature of turnkey adoption of the 'centralized' technologies of multinational firms, nor to the neoclassical notion of technologies molding themselves to local factor prices; the real process is much more complex. There is little doubt that the equipment and technological practices used in much of the formal sector in developing countries are imported or copied from the more advanced economies, where they were originally developed for domestic use.

It may be possible, however, that Third World countries have access to a range of readily available techniques, in the form of next-to-new vintages, and as such they may potentially have a wider range of technological choice with respect to industry than is generally admitted. But there is a great deal of misunderstanding about these secondhand technologies. They are only useful for a developing country (that is, a country with significantly different factor proportions, especially a labor surplus, than a developed country) if their replacement in the developed economy was triggered, neoclassical style, by increases in the wage–interest ratio, that is, where the increase in the capital–labor ratio of the newer technique is caused by a rising wage trend in the advanced economies. If this were the motive for developing these technologies, then the secondhand machines might incorporate a factor ratio that more closely approximates the proportions of the borrowing country. As noted, to the contrary, it is highly probable that firms in industrial economies develop technologies principally in response to opportunities for exploiting dynamic scale economies. This implies—very critically—that in addition to current techniques, much of the next-to-new market will also be factor inefficient in borrowing countries. Particularly in the production of standardized consumer and intermediate goods, and in the process industries, the 'price sensitive range' between available techniques is small (Vieira da Cunha, 1983).

Indeed, it has been shown that the

"capital intensity of multinationals in Brazil was not a result of government [price] policy .... The firms tended to replicate plants producing at the same scale elsewhere, and it is doubtful that they would have modified plant design merely in response to a different set of factor prices" (Morley and Smith, 1977, page 260).

Neoclassical economists generally argue that high capital-labor ratios are caused by 'distorted' factor prices (principally through minimum-wage laws), whereas the appropriate technologists generally attribute the capital intensity of Third World enterprises to government policies favoring large firms. In *both* cases, however, the goal is to make capital more like putty, or to mold it to the existing factor proportions of each economy. I have suggested that this is not the way that industrial capital works in the real world. The only alternative in the consumer durables and process industries is for developing countries to invent their own technologies. But it would very likely be more costly for them to develop these technologies than it is to import them, and the cost of development would likely have enormously distorting effects on those economies (such as income concentration at a scale now unimaginable).

Appropriate technology strategies are really designed to alter dramatically the composition of outputs; that is, they are about *different* industries, not simply different technologies *within* the modern industries. In this sense, appropriate technology strategies would reverse the effects of import-substitution policies, whose main effect was to introduce change in the composition of domestically available goods in the Brazilian economy and, *as a consequence of this compositional change*, to alter the technological bias of the industrial structure. At this point, we are no longer discussing the alternative technological and spatial forms that modern industry may take, but the different technological and locational logics of industrialization versus 'protoindustrialization'.[21] This may be fine for the most impoverished

----

[21] 'Appropriate technologies' strategies also include the 'rural bias' programs suggested by Lipton (1977) and others. Lipton argues that a unit of investment applied to rural areas and agricultural activities produces more output and income in many countries than it would in modern urban industries and infrastructure.

regions of many countries, but it has little application to a regional development program for already-industrial economies such as Brazil, Mexico, and Korea.

This discussion of technologies is still too limited. Industrialization does not involve the simple static matching of discrete technologies to individual outputs; it involves a social organization of labor among firms and thus, significant sharing of technologies ('joint production' in economics terminology). Think back to all the reasons for vertical and horizontal disintegration of production elaborated in chapters 2 and 3. Even if the firms involved in these systems use imported technologies, *the production system as a whole may enjoy significant flexibility by virtue of the structure of interfirm transactions and the technology sharing it implies*.

Even when a production system is marked by the installation of 'turnkey' final assembly plants (as is frequently the case in Brazil and Mexico), the production system for inputs may still be tailored to the local environment in important ways. High levels of firm specialization and complicated patterns of interfirm and intersectoral linkages imply the existence of types of scale and input flexibility not captured by conventional thinking about the individual firm and/or product. It cannot be known, in principle, exactly what production techniques these intermediate input suppliers will use. They may range from large-scale supplier contractors—as in firms that make auto parts in Brazil—to specialized but flexible customizers of capital goods inputs or final outputs.[22] The range of techniques at this intermediate level is much greater than that found in the final output firms in consumer durables or process industries (Addis, 1988).

---

[21] (continued)
There is obviously significant merit to his criticism of the lack of attention paid to agriculture and rural incomes. On the other hand, there is remarkably little evidence that investments in agriculture, even if statically more efficient, are dynamically more efficient than urban–industrial investments, even in labor-surplus economies. For the problem over the medium and long runs is not absolute levels of income, but mobilizing some portion of that income for investment. Industry is generally best at this, for technical reasons, having to do with its propensity to enjoy scale economies and a higher rate of technical dynamism than agriculture.

It should also be made clear that this does not imply that a country can go ahead with industrialization and urbanization without first securing adequate levels of agricultural production and rural incomes. History suggests that these features are necessary for successful urbanization and industrialization (see section 5.2). The point is simply that Lipton's point should not be read without care; a rural bias strategy is not a replacement for urbanization, but a moment in one process of economic development involving city and country, industry and agriculture.

[22] The absurdity of Pigou's "lake" of intermediate inputs should also now be apparent. When external economies of scale are recognized, the intermediate level of production becomes the most important, as economists from Smith through Marx and Sraffa have recognized.

All this is another way of saying that the big visible factories in São Paulo are only the tip of the iceberg of its industrial economy. The region contains a rich stock of organizational complexities. It is a gigantic interlocked production complex with substantial participation of small and medium sized firms, national and local capital, as well as large firms and multinational capital. Small and medium sized firms and local capital, moreover, are not isolated into different sectors, strictly separated from the modern industries, as is claimed in many 'dualist' interpretations of the industrial economy. They are vertically and horizontally intertwined (Portes and Benton, 1984).

Consider, now, the implications of this reasoning. Industrialization that achieves the implantation of input-producing complexes actually might adapt the scale of production to the conditions of the country's markets to a greater extent than would be implied if one simply took stock of the use of imported technologies or the technical structure of final output plants. This is because elaborate industrial complexes are an expression of a certain level of *organizational de*centralization and thus organizational *flexibility* in production. To some extent, the spatial concentration of these industrial complexes is the correlate of their organizational complexity. A Rostovian big push strategy, by contrast, would substitute spatial decentralization via organizational centralization (the big plant of the big firm) for the organizational complexity but spatial concentration of an industrial pole like São Paulo.

Let us turn from these mesoeconomic considerations to the macroeconomic correlates of different approaches to the initiation of industrialization. If a big push strategy is opted for, macroeconomic demand constraints to development appear very rapidly; as noted, it has been impossible even for the biggest Third World economies to overcome these demand limitations. If a protoindustrial strategy is attempted, on the other hand, it is not clear that scale effects are created. The developing country might invest its scarce capital in handicraft industries, with an eye toward limited, 'sensitive' modernization, but if returns to scale are absent, either profits have to be very low or wages very low. If the latter, then demand does not materialize to push further investment; if the former, then the initial investment of capital may generate no further capital accumulation and the industry will stagnate or may even deteriorate when the rate of capital accumulation is insufficient to maintain the initial investment. The development of a set of elaborately interlinked production firms, on the other hand, suggests the possibility of minimizing both supply and demand constraints. On the supply side, it creates dynamic increasing returns through external economies. On the demand side, it reduces the absolute levels of efficient output relative to what would be required by 'full' modernization of the big push (that is, fully integrated) type.

This is not to say that Brazil, or any other rapidly industrializing Third World economy, has actually followed the latter path completely.

Most existing semi-industrialized economies appear to display curious mixes of the three alternatives discussed here, and reflect them in the spatial form that industrialization has taken. Brazilian industrialization, for example, is the product of an attempted big push, but which (perhaps unintentionally) has come to rely on a flexibly specialized, vertically disintegrated industrial division of labor in many industries. Brazil may have attempted excessive vertical integration (with participation of multinational firms) in some sectors relative to what could have been done efficiently through an industrial system based on closely linked medium sized firms.

The demand for spatial concentration associated with industrialization depends on the particular scale of production along with the sectoral mix, and their combined effects on the social division of labor. The analysis in chapter 5 suggests that spatial polarization can be most successfully reduced in Brazil through distribution-led growth. Realistically, however, this is not likely to occur in the immediate future, and the Brazilian economy will continue to be plagued by high levels of intertemporal uncertainty, and sluggish growth of poorly distributed consumer income. As such, it will continue to industrialize with dense interfirm relations, high levels of organizational disintegration in the production of intermediate inputs, low levels of labor absorption in the final output stages of production, and resulting tendencies toward spatial polarization. But, as this discussion of technology and macroeconomics suggests, the response is not to cast aside modern industry, but instead to ask whether a country such as Brazil can form a polycentric regional system of production centers without losing the external economies of scale, interfirm specialization, and production system flexibilities which I have described. External economies here refers both to comparative statics (productivity, due to flexibility and specialization of firms and ease of interconnection) and to dynamics (innovation, redivision of labor, skill transmission). Since these latter features are key to the overall (nonspatial) outcomes of development, such as employment and income generation through productivity increases, the question becomes whether these goals could be realized in a form other than São Paulo as, for example, in a set of smaller, but linked, complexes. I suggest, in chapters to come, that the answer may be yes, but that regional economic policies will require a great deal more sophistication than they have had historically if such a goal is to be reached.

6.2 Do polarization and industrialization strangle other regions, or: do centers cause peripheries?

It has been argued frequently that regional inequalities, by definition, provoke social inequalities, that is, distortions in the eventual pattern of economic development in a country with great regional inequalities. More importantly, it is also often implied that industrial regions are somehow directly responsible for the problems of peripheral regions or rural areas. Cities are characterized as parasites, stealing human and physical resources from other regions and especially from the countryside. Industrial polarization is said to be associated with 'urban bias' in development, and it is labelled a cause for underdevelopment of other parts of the country. Since these kinds of accusations frequently weigh very heavily in policy debates and in regional political rivalries within developing countries, they merit evaluation within the framework articulated above.

To put the analytical issues as clearly as possible, we must ask whether observed differences in development levels *between* regions are caused by the interconnections between regions—in the sense that developed regions *cause* the problems of less developed regions—or whether each set of regional successes and problems is primarily attributable either to the models of development used *within* each of them or to the *national* model of economic development as a whole (and not simply its spatial aspects). To answer this question, we must separate out at least four major dimensions of regional development in semi-industrialized economies, dimensions which are frequently lumped together in the heat of the debate.

First, any process of transition from a rural and subsistence economy to an industrial economy is linked to the creation of levels of social inequality greater than exist normally in a rural, small producer economy (but not greater than are found generally in a feudal or *latifundista* economy). These inequalities result from the simple fact that the division of labor in any industrial economy—whether capitalist or socialist—is more complex than the division of labor in an agrarian economy (Kuznets, 1955). The greater the division of functions in an economy, the greater the inter-occupational dispersion of income, ceteris paribus. Socialist economies minimize this dispersion, whereas capitalist economies tend to exaggerate it well beyond its technical bases (because of concentration of wealth, and because of more pronounced occupational disparities).[23] This social inequality in the course of development usually takes on a spatial appearance, that is, urban–rural average income differentials. But there is nothing in this logic to indicate that rural incomes are actually depressed by industrialization and urbanization, only that gaps open up. There is nothing identifiably causal in the relationship.

A second, more powerful, version of the argument asserts that urbanization and industrialization actually reduce the developmental potential of non-urban areas and peripheral regions. There are several ways in which this is said to occur. It is argued that industrial regions 'pull' migrants from the countryside, thus depleting them of their major resources, which are labor and human knowledge. Note that the explanation for backwardness of other areas is directly located in the spatial relations of these regions to more advanced areas. This view is based on a misreading of the Harris–Todaro

---

[23] Investment income versus wage income refers to the 'functional' distribution of income whereas occupational disparities and functional disparities both contribute to inequality of the 'size' distribution of income, that is, its overall magnitude. The difference is between 'whom' and 'how much'.

urban–rural migration model. The model itself does not specify 'first causes', that is, whether the flow of migrants toward cities is a result of push effects or pull effects. Yet, as we saw in chapter 5, the problem is clearly that of push, because of the shortage of rural incomes. We have already established that rural labor supplies to urban areas are highly elastic, even though urban labor demand is relatively inelastic at a given output level. Whether supply elasticity is caused by push or pull thus turns on whether rural incomes are 'low' or urban incomes are 'high'. In general, urban wage increases in manufacturing industries in countries such as Brazil have not kept pace, over the last thirty years, with productivity increases (Bacha, 1978). It is unlikely that in any capitalist economy, whether developed or Third World, productivity increases will be fully passed through to workers, even after netting out the costs of capital replacement. In the developed economies, however, productivity increases have often been shared between capitalists and workers, leading simultaneously to an increase in the real product wage and to capital accumulation. Only if wages had risen in real product terms would it be possible to attribute migration to 'high' urban salary levels. In Brazil, even though real wage rates in urban areas remain above those in rural areas, the ratio between the two has tended to remain stable since the initial gaps were opened up in the early stages of industrialization. Thus, it is analytically wrong to claim that migration is primarily a 'pull' phenomenon. In semi-industrialized countries such as Brazil, the primary cause of migration can be assigned to the lack of income opportunities in rural areas; a *push* effect. Rural incomes are so low that people go to the cities looking for work, even though urban wages are not very high relative to the cost of living in the large cities and industrial productivity, and there are high rates of unemployment. In other words, the depletion of rural population is a consequence of the form of development that occurs in rural areas, and not precisely the effects that urban–industrial development has on rural–urban relations: cities can only extract human resources from the countryside to the extent that the economy of the latter pushes them towards the cities.

There are two aspects of interregional *relations*, however, that act to distance the fates of industrializing regions from all other regions—urban and rural alike—of the national territory. The first of these has already been noted: in the early stages of industrialization, once a set of productive forces takes root at any specified set of locations, the developmental trajectories of industrial systems help to consolidate those locations as the privileged geographical loci of the emergent industrial economy (see section 3.1) . Initially, industries have a 'window of locational opportunity', but as they generate their own agglomeration economies, the window rapidly closes around a limited number of locations. It only reopens as a consequence of the dynamic growth processes which bring into the economy whole new dominant production ensembles. How and why some places develop expanding industrial complexes whereas others move along different developmental trajectories has by no means been solved at the level of theory.

Theoretical conclusions should not be hastily drawn from this point, however. Even though it is true that agglomeration forecloses opportunities for other areas—that is, industrialization cannot take place evenly, everywhere at once—it cannot be asserted that, therefore, the underdevelopment or stagnation of these areas is caused by polarization in dynamic industrial regions. Agglomeration economies are not strictly *allocational* in nature. They arise endogenously in the course of economic *growth*. They do not simply put a predefined set of activities in a place; they also form part of its developmental dynamic. With increasing returns to scale, industrialization is not a zero-sum game. The simple spatial redistribution of activity would very likely produce a national economy whose whole is less than the sum of its parts, whereas, as we have seen, agglomeration arises as part of a growth process which is exactly the opposite. What this means is that the creation of large centers may generate resources for the national economy which cannot be had in its absence, even while they open up major gaps in welfare levels between places.

The problem is that we actually do not know to what extent the generation of this type of economic dynamism and greater interregional distribution of its benefits are mutually exclusive. The question is manifestly not whether peripheral areas could do better at local development if they did not have to compete with the great industrial centers; this question incorrectly assumes that the static effects of reducing interregional competition prove the case for reducing it. Rarely does the regional development literature— in spite of the appellation 'development'—consider the future development paths of the places benefitted by redistribution of activity and their relationships to the future of the national economy. *The appropriate question is whether a country can industrialize with a polycentric regional system of production centers and maintain the benefits of scale and specialization which are key to modern industrial growth.* I have suggested that this issue cannot be skirted by proposing alternative technologies, but must be confronted directly at the level of the spatial divisibility of modern forces of production, given their technological, organizational and spatial characteristics.

6.2.1 Other dimensions of rural–urban relations

Urban–industrial regions are also said to restrict the development of other regions in the national economy by virtue of the 'food–wages' connection. Many countries, Brazil included, have adopted agricultural policies that depress the price of basic food commodities, apparently in an effort to insure a supply of cheap food in their industrial cities (de Janvry, 1981). Undoubtedly, this depresses the potential incomes of food producers and prevents them from raising productivity and incomes. In Brazil, where rapid agricultural modernization has been under way since the early 1970s, rising agricultural productivity has been strongly concentrated on large landholdings and mostly realized in the production of nonfood crops or those aimed at export markets (CEDEPLAR, 1986).

Urban wages, as noted, are indeed so low that urban workers would be in general hard put to pay much more for their food needs (Homem de Melo, 1986). The prices paid by the urban sector to the rural food-producing sector, then, do maintain rural incomes at a level lower than if, for example, urban wages were higher and urban workers could thus afford more for food. But this impediment to development of the rural small producer economy is not caused by polarization or urbanization per se, but rather by the income and land-distribution structures that exist in rural areas themselves and cheap food prices. This is obvious from a counterfactual question: if urban workers did not exist to be fed, at any price, would small producers in rural areas of Brazil be better off? It is probable that these small producers would be at subsistence.

Some rural areas and some rural interests of Brazil are of course distinctly linked to industrialization and urbanization: those that produce foodstuffs for the urban middle and upper classes; or those that use agroindustrial inputs, or those that produce export crops designed to earn credits in the nation's external accounts. All of this describes agriculture in the Southeast and South of Brazil, and certain areas of the Center-West. These sectors are dominated by large producers (with the exception of Santa Catarina), who have a virtual monopoly on landownership suitable for many of these activities, as well as the credit and capital required to produce in these markets competitively. Concomitantly, small producers are excluded or driven out of these areas.

These agricultural *regions* cannot be called underdeveloped. They are rather highly developed, but at the expense of the small producer. They repeat the distributional and productivity patterns of the urban–industrial centers in rural activities. The question is whether these precise outcomes—'good' and 'bad'—are caused by industrialization and polarization per se, or caused by the particular model of agriculture, land distribution, and economic development generally chosen in these countries, in addition to the obvious political and economic weakness of the small agricultural producers. If the relationship is only a general and aggregated one, that is, through the circuits of product demand and the balance of payments, then to attempt to change the distributional and productive structure of agriculture by reducing urban–industrial development is (as Edgar Hoover once so aptly put it) "like using a shotgun to kill flies." It would be better to deal with agriculture and land distribution directly.

The final argument which attributes rural or peripheral backwardness to industrialization and polarization holds that these processes divert the political attention of the state away from rural areas and agriculture, while simultaneously tying up limited capital resources in urbanization and industrialization and thus starving the rural sector of capital. Obviously, the extent to which this is true differs widely from country to country. Let us just take the case of Brazil. It could hardly be argued that rural areas, agricultural activities, or peripheral regions have lacked political attention: they have been the focus of dozens of development programs since the late 1950s (de Oliveira, 1977). Indeed, it could be argued that peripheral regions occupy an excessively large place in the national political discourse of Brazil, almost to the detriment of other ostensibly nonregional but equally pressing development issues. Nor is it easy to demonstrate that any of these areas or activities have lacked capital or incentives. Both the government and the private sector have made massive investments in agriculture, rural areas, and peripheral regions; $14 billion in Amazonian *infrastructure* and credits alone in the 1970s and early 1980s (Hecht, 1986). Arguably, they have been the *wrong* expenditures, but the point remains that, even in a country which has followed a fast-growth industrialization and urbanization strategy, there is no necessary zero-sum game with other regions and activities. Indeed, it could be argued that much of the redistributive power of the national state comes precisely from surpluses generated in its urban activities.

6.3 Can polarized activity be redistributed?
In practice, much of regional policy in Brazil has consisted of attempts to redistribute economic activity in space (de Oliveira, 1977). The principal vehicle for explicit regional policy has been the planned urban–industrial growth pole, whose purpose is to redistribute and disperse polarization impulses. It is well known that these policies have, for the most part, failed. By understanding why they have failed, however, we can gain some new insights into the specific nature of polarization and the forces that encourage it.

The original growth-pole idea, from Perroux (1950), identified a complex and—it should be added—eclectic set of forces that induce a dynamic kind of imbalance in the economy. Growth was supposed to fill in the imbalances. Perroux drew the latter notion directly from Schumpeter (1934) and Joan Robinson (who remarked in the early 1950s that growth is like "lurching from one state of disequilibrium to another"). Note that the original idea was not *spatial*; it was simply an attempt to abandon equilibrium concepts of growth and development and replace them with a development theory based on concrete notions about technology and industrial organization. After the initial publication of Perroux's ideas on economic space, both Myrdal (1957) and then Hirschman's work on national development in 1958 (which contained some remarks on interregional growth transmission) began (perhaps unwittingly) to transform the Perrouxian concept in two critical ways: it was regionalized, and it was developed into a planning tool as well as a theory about the actual process of economic development. In the course of this transformation, a number of the flaws or vague areas of the original concept were magnified and some new problems were introduced.

First, Perroux's idea that the process of imbalanced growth centered around a propulsive force was extremely vague and eclectically formulated in the original. The idea was that the propulsive force could make things happen in the economy around it by causing upstream or downstream activities to be established. Perroux's original language, however, did not specify exactly *how* the propulsion would be effected. His grab bag of ideas included many different processes: induced innovation; innovation diffusion; the power of oligopolistic firms to command an input–output structure; and so on. This left the field open for his interpreters to identify, incorrectly, the propulsive force as the 'lead firm' or unit of the large corporation.

Second, it really is not evident that Perroux intended his concept of polarization to be spatial, and even less clear that he believed it could operate at the subnational level (de Bresson, 1986). Hirschman (1958) recognized this ambiguity, noting that subnational regions could not be selectively 'closed' like national economies. When Perroux wrote of 'points' of growth and selective 'channels' of growth, he was referring to the *organizational characteristics* of economic and technological spaces rather than to geographical spaces of economic growth.

Notwithstanding these problems, the idea of planned urban–industrial growth poles became a fixture of the regional development literature by the early 1960s. In the planned-growth-pole literature, two dominant assumptions crystallized out of the original terminology. The first was that propulsive units were to be large, oligopolistic industries with complex input–output relations. The second was that these input–output relations would not only be induced by the organizational pole, but that they would agglomerate around that pole, in space. We should note that the planning and geography literature is full of much cruder versions of growth-pole analysis which omit the mediation of industrial systems altogether, depicting place-poles as attracting other place-poles (Boudeville, 1966; Gore, 1984; Nichols, 1969; Parr, 1973). From these assumptions, countries such as Brazil undertook large programs of installing state-run industries in peripheral regions, or offering large inventives to private industries to do the same (SUDENE is the classic example, in the post-1964 period).

The nearly complete failure of these programs is by now well known: despite very considerable investments, they have had very low returns in terms of job creation, increases in local per-capita income, and spin-off effects into the local industrial economy (de Oliveira, 1977). This applies not only to Third World countries, but to underdeveloped regions in developed economies, such as Italy's Mezzogiorno (Martinelli, 1986). Why? Urban–industrial growth poles based on the installation of large factories in peripheral regions are really attempts to invert—in time and space—the spatial development process described in chapters 2 and 3.

In time, they would do so by starting with the large plant rather than the developing social division of labor. In space, they initially would isolate the large unit from any set of external economies. Their failure thus lies principally in their rudimentary comprehension of the division of labor in industry. Perroux, like Schumpeter and Robinson before him, was referring to the developmental dynamic between points in the economy, whereas planners took that idea and looked at the large *existing* volume of input–output transactions of oligopolistic plants and assumed that such a transactional structure could be easily developed at or transferred to assigned points in regional space. The planning concept completely failed to take into account that in many areas developed input–output relations are the outcome of densely articulated industrial systems which have high levels of spatial inertia because of their external economies. They are not easily transferred across space. Alternatively, planners failed to realize that oligopolistic industries are least likely to induce spatial polarization of industrial activity. The high levels of vertical integration of the large, technologically mature, vertically integrated industrial plant depress the level of external transactions required and thus the dependence on the local industrial milieu. Moreover, a high proportion of the external transactions they require do not have to take place between units located in the same region, for their transactional relationships tend to be routinized and large in scale. It is thus extremely unlikely that they could create the kind of complex organizational and labor-market dynamics in the locality that lead to the creation of local spin-off firms, entrepreneurial development, skill transmission, and so on. It is not surprising that urban–industrial growth poles have simply created branch-plant outposts in peripheral regions.

Growth poles were also justified through non-Perrouxian neoclassical reasoning. We have already addressed, in some detail, the problems with any factor–price model of agglomeration which ignores the structure of production (sections 2.3 and 3.2). Beyond those standard problems, many neoclassical economists attempted to justify growth poles by claiming that intertemporal uncertainty played a critical role in polarization. Taking their cue from Hotelling's early model of duopoly, they argued that, under conditions of rapid economic growth, unusually high levels of uncertainty about markets were created, impeding decentralization behavior. Growth-pole policies, in essence, could provide the conditions of certainty that would permit decentralization of industry. We need only refer back to the argument in section 3.2, which suggests that uncertainty plays a central role in the determination of the division of labor and, hence, locational behavior. But it suggests, likewise, that such uncertainty cannot be addressed at the level of spatial behavior, because the latter is largely an outcome rather than a cause.

Growth poles are not simply failures of a dream, however. They may have actively regressive effects. This can best be understood through a concrete example. A major Brazilian textile manufacturer recently established a large production complex in Natal, in the Northeast of Brazil. This was the firm's first complex outside of its traditional center, the city of Blumenau in the state of Santa Catarina. The complex was established with incentives from SUDENE, and involves both the farms that produce cotton and the industrial operations of spinning and weaving. The firm admits that without incentives it never would have located any industrial operations in the Northeast. With incentives, however, the firm admits that it is paying only 60% of the hourly wages it pays in the South for the same work (personal communication, 1986). Beyond the savings on wage costs (part of which the firm admits are offset by low quality and productivity in the Northeast), the firm is happy to say that the example of locating production outside the South has chilled demands for wage increases by its highly productive workers in Santa Catarina. In other words, geographical redistribution can be used as a means to accomplish nonspatial goals. Remembering our analysis of the wages – growth connection (chapter 5), we can easily see that the diversion of investments away from existing industrial centers and toward peripheral regions reduces the growth of labor demand in the centers. By weakening the bargaining power of urban workers, regional policy becomes, in effect, a spatial wage-reduction policy (see Storper, 1984).

Many of the failures of development strategies in the industrializing Third World do, indeed, have sources that take particular and differentiated spatial or regional *forms*, as in the cases of low rural incomes, rural – urban migration, and so on. But it would be illogical to assume that these developmental problems can be eliminated simply by reducing one of their *outcomes*, interregional polarization. Continued polarization is evidence of problems that can only be resolved through development policies, which may in turn be targeted to regions to the extent that the problems to be solved are regionally concentrated.

There is a broader implication of this reasoning for regional development policy. It cannot be assumed that regional policy should have as its goal the elimination of interregional inequalities. Even though the failure of an industrializing economy to reduce polarization is evidence of development problems, there is nothing in this reasoning which says that the solution of those problems comes specifically through the elimination of interregional inequalities. Polarization per se, as I have pointed out, is not a problem from the strictly economic standpoint. As Gore points out, to assume that a reduction in interregional inequality is equivalent to a reduction in interpersonal inequality is to commit an ecological fallacy (1984, page 53). Thus, there is no reason that spatial or regional equilibrium should be privileged as the goal of economic policy, unless we can demonstrate that it would necessarily bring more development, more welfare, or more human satisfaction than could be had in its absence.

Regional development policy 1: getting the domestic factor markets right

It should by now be evident that the causes of polarization are not strictly local; polarization is an outcome of deep-seated political and economic features of the *national* pathway to industrialization. This pathway is built from two basic elements: on the one hand, the shape and functioning of factor markets and the incentives they provide to decisionmakers, and, on the other, the concrete strategies and policies employed with respect to the technological and organizational features of the industrial system itself. Successful development policies must address both these elements and their geographical causes and outcomes. In this chapter I address the former; in the following chapter I will take up the latter.

The major problem with factor markets, as we saw in chapter 5, is the production and reproduction of labor surplus, and its close relationship to the macroeconomic problems of stagnation and uncertainty which strongly encourage polarization. I now suggest two components of national economic policy—one 'urban' and the other 'rural'— designed to alter the shape of labor markets and thus the macroeconomy. Section 7.1 provides a more thorough defense of the notion that rising urban incomes are key to growth and its polarization-reducing potential. In section 7.2 I argue that an appropriate *rural* development policy is the only feasible way to reduce the elasticity of urban labor supplies and thus to attenuate the downward pressure on wages in urban labor markets.

7.1 Urbanization and the interregional mobility of industry

It is now clear that the main direct route to depolarization of industry in a developing country with an intermediate level of industrialization and per-capita income is not massive spatial redistribution of that industry, but the establishment of a *macroeconomic* process that allows decentralization to take place through three concrete mechanisms: (1) the installation of new sectors, which then generate agglomerated territorial growth centers; (2) scale increases in existing industries and the creation of growth peripheries; (3) the 'pushing' of both of the above by the inducement of agglomeration diseconomies in urban labor markets. The macroeconomic model depends in general on changes in urban wage determination and thus, on the distribution of income.

Recall that this macroeconomic analysis (in section 5.1), was elucidated via a comparison of underdeveloped with developed economies. Comparative statics, as I have emphasized throughout, are always a poor replacement for dynamic analysis, and conclusions derived from the former but applied to the latter are often wrong in economic history. Before we get directly to the specific role that urban areas play in income distribution, then, it is first necessary to establish in a bit more detail the case for rising wage income as the foundation of development.

It has frequently been argued that it is necessary to concentrate income in developing economies in order to create industrial markets because the rich have a higher marginal propensity to consume industrial goods than the poor. Industrialized production permits high productivity levels, and, to the extent that consumption is limited to the rich, prices and are more elastic, thus raising profit rates, which in turn sustain the investment requirements for continued expansion of the economy (see Bacha, 1978; Harrod, 1973; Kalecki, 1971). Note that this is not the conventional neoconservative argument based on the propensity to *save* on the part of the rich, but instead on their propensity to consume and to invest. It follows that, to initiate modern industrialization, income concentration is required to establish the class of consumers. It is for this reason that much industrialization in the Third World has been condemned as inherently attached to intolerable levels of inequality.

Whether or not we accept this reasoning, increasing income inequality in the course of industrialization is a fact of life in the semi-industrialized economies. The question now is whether extremely high levels of income concentration *continue* to provide the grounds for growth once the initial phase of installing modern industry has been realized or whether such concentration then *impedes* further expansion possibilities. To answer this question we must look at the mix of goods that promotes growth, and the income distribution that accompanies such a production – consumption profile.

Modern, technically sophisticated industrial goods are, in effect, luxury goods in developing economies, that is, the province of a restricted number of consumers. Yet these same goods—such as consumer durables and sophisticated capital goods—are known as 'mass-consumption' and 'mass-production' items in the developed countries. In terms of basic technological potential, they are amenable to high productivity levels and price reductions when they are mass produced, whereas 'luxury goods' in a developed economy refers to items that generally are *not* amenable to mass production and therefore remain expensive because of their artisanal content. This is exactly the opposite of the situation in a Third World economy.

The argument in favor of long-run income concentration is that, even though the rich saturate their demands for existing luxury goods at a certain point, they can easily move on to other luxury goods. The economy grows fastest this way because the rich continue to have a higher marginal propensity to consume than other classes and can afford to pay luxury premiums in any case. If this is true, then redistributing incomes would in fact not induce as much growth as continuation of income concentration. The basic principle is that growth must produce income redistribution (as in the bell curves) and not the other way around.

Actually, there is very ample reason to believe otherwise. First, it is very probable that the rich in countries such as Brazil have actually shifted out of the first type of 'luxury goods', that is, of the mass-production type, and are devoting very considerable shares of their income to the second type, that is, the kind that is not easily amenable to productivity increases. In other words, the rich are devoting much of their consumption power to goods with high artisanal content, having reached a point of satisfying their mass production requirements. This is evident in the degree of speculation in real estate and luxury apartments, luxury clothes, and travel in most of Latin America, and the slow rates of expansion of the mass production industries. Even though some of this luxury consumption is linked to mass production—as in apartments that require refrigerators—it is a heavy price to pay for that mass production. The heavily speculative nature of many of these economies suggests that existing savings cannot find solid investment opportunities and that a lowering of profit rates and redistribution of income would actually not be met with less investment, but with more.

Second, efficiency itself—as should be clear from the analysis of the social division of labor—is a highly dynamic result of the process of industrial capital accumulation. In some countries, such as Argentina, domestic markets are not large enough to support efficient production in many modern industries, however that production might be organized. But in the large countries such as Brazil, it is probable that potential productivity is not being maximized. Overall expansion of industrial output would permit productivity increases even in the very largest of existing industries, such as automobiles.

Third, the marginal propensity to consume is not necessarily a linear function of absolute income level. Were the poor to get richer, their marginal propensities to consume would very likely change progressively in the direction of the propensities of the rich. Thus, even though the initial effects of income redistribution might be slow, they would likely increase *at an increasing rate*.

The central point is that *once* an economy reaches an intermediate stage of development, a set of *qualitative* changes in consumption propensities and production efficiencies may be possible that are simply not taken into account by many of the conventional analyses of economic systems. This is especially true of input–output analysis of those economies, particularly if technology is held constant and analysis is restricted to the plant or industry level.

Thus, changes in the wage structure of the economy are key to achieving the kind of macroeconomic development that can reverse interregional polarization. Since most of the wages in these economies are urban, this implies *changes in urban wages as a key to inducing growth and polarization reversal*. It is very unlikely, however, that changes in urban wage levels are going to be achieved directly by state decrees in countries such as Brazil.

For one thing, it is improbable that an immediate and dramatic policy of raising salaries would succeed politically; it is difficult to 'get the price right' for urban labor through decree because capitalists respond by with-holding investment, and this reduces the effectiveness of the policy (for example, as in 1986 during the Brazilian *Plano Cruzado*).

Realistically, it is necessary to let urban salaries develop through a political process of negotiation between workers and employers, that is, with freedom for urban workers to organize themselves in their work-places and in their urban communities. Therefore, if spatial redistribution of industry is used as a way to reduce labor-market tightness in highly developed industrial regions, or as a threat *against* workers' unions, or as a way to promote labor mobility so as to break up stable, organized groups of urban workers, then it is economically and socially counterproductive (Storper, 1984).[24] At the very least, economic policies should not be biased against the positive effects of spatial concentration, and spatial policy should certainly not be used as a cover for other goals. A great deal more investigation—taking into account microeconomic and macro-economic relationships, as well as the historical and political contexts of economic events—is called for in order to formulate spatial policies which are more sensitive to these social foundations of development processes.

7.2 Rural development: changing the elasticity of urban labor supplies

There is ample historical and econometric evidence to suggest that the existence of relatively high rural incomes before, or in the early phases of, industrialization will slow migratory flows toward cities and affect urban wage determination in a positive way (Evans, 1987; Lo and Salih, 1981). Particularly when this type of agricultural development is coupled to full employment, urban firms are forced to offer relatively high salaries in order to attract labor from the countryside. In consequence, the consump-tion power of the urban masses tends to grow, fueling macroeconomic expansion and the eventual attainment of greater efficiencies in industrial production. As a result of this macroeconomic growth, the economy should develop intersectoral diversity and create strong diseconomies of agglomeration in its centers, while at the same time generating labor-market formation in a variety of places through high rates of labor

[24] Only with a certain degree of spatial stability (that is, in their communities) is it likely that solidaristic communities of workers capable of advancing the economic interests of workers in urban labor markets will develop. It should be noted that these communities are characterized by high levels of in-migration and out-migration, and a great deal of diversity in the origins of urban migrants—a long literature exists on this subject in Brazil today. And a long literature on 19th and early 20th century working-class communities in the USA suggests that community stability over at least one generation is an important precondition for significant collective gains in political wage-setting processes).

absorption. Thus, the system of industrial cities and regions would tend to become extended, reducing polarization. Compared with the five bell shapes of modernization theory, the critical difference here is that the rural–urban population shift is slowed first, and the reduction of geographical polarization is an outcome.

The theoretical argument in favor of using an agricultural development strategy in this manner refers to the relationships of output, capital, and income in agricultural production as compared with urban industry. Put bluntly, industrialization in general presupposes higher levels of capital resources than agriculture, and it is less flexible over time with respect to capitalization levels than agriculture. At subsistence, agriculture uses little capital and has steeply diminishing returns. But with applications of capital, returns can rise rapidly and with them, real incomes. The capital can be applied gradually, in stages. What originally serves for subsistence can become a source of wealth. To the extent that the distribution of land does not change radically in the process, but only the application of capital, incomes rise *without massive income concentration*. Industry, on the other hand, often requires large, indivisible blocks of capital that almost necessarily implies property concentration. The distribution of income in a fully industrial economy, however, is mediated by labor markets as well as by property ownership because much income is paid out in the form of wages. That is why we pay so much attention here to urban labor markets.

The policy question becomes whether the theoretical possibility of forming a 'virtuous circle' between agriculture and urban labor markets can actually be realized. Although innumerable points of contention on this issue remain, there is substantial agreement that no inexorable, natural path out of subsistence and toward Jeffersonian-style smallholding, modern agriculture exists.[25]

---

[25] The European feudalism debate is of limited use for our purposes, however theoretically engaging it might be. This is because the question it takes up is not the problem of overcoming subsistence. Feudal lords had already done that. That debate concerns why feudalism broke down and led to urbanization and industrialization (see Brenner, 1977). No virtuous circle was formed: after the enclosures, English cities were flooded with labor, very much replicating labor-market conditions found in contemporary Third World cities. The conditions were not as dire over the long run in England, however, because England came to dominate world industrial markets. This strategy, duplicated today by Japan, is hardly feasible for countries such as Brazil. Their resolution of the labor-absorption problem must be based on a more modest role in the world economy.

The 19th century North American case has some suggestions for strategy, in that it combined land distribution to a large number of farmers with the steady development of export markets. The one principal structural difference, of course, is that small American farmers were not forced to compete, within their own country, with highly capitalized large farming operations, as they are in contemporary Brazil. And there was no traditional subsistence sector to 'reform' as there is in many Third World nations. This is especially a problem in areas with high population densities or extreme poverty.

Thus, two factors are isolated: on one hand, the impulse to capital accumulation; on the other, the distribution of income, which is closely associated with the distribution of land, ceteris paribus. *Latifundia* may accumulate capital, but they will not do well at distributing income and they tend to expel people into urban labor markets as they mechanize, whereas small farms without export markets usually stay in subsistence. *A developmentalist path lies somewhere between the two*, in that it creates the possibility of raising rural incomes to the point that urban activities must use greater wage incentives to find their labor supplies. In this analysis, rural development is as much a means to national development as it is narrowly a strategy for rural development.

Much of the current regional development debate rejects the argument presented here. It implies that development of rural and peripheral regions is not a way station to industrialization, but the primary goal of development strategies (Lipton, 1977; Stöhr and Taylor, 1979; Stöhr and Todtling, 1979). That is, rural development is represented as a *replacement* for urban industrialization. One reason for this was already pointed out in chapter 6: the distaste for increases in social inequalities that usually accompany industrialization.

The replacement of polarized urban and industrial development would be accomplished by a variety of means, including 'selective spatial closure' and the diversion of investments to agriculture rather than industry, or at the least to industrial activities located at the local level and linked to agricultural activities. Several significant problems can be noted in light of the analysis put forth in this book. First, selective spatial closure makes it very difficult to have access to the product export markets which in turn permit rising rural incomes. Autarchy and subsistence are, historically, very closely linked. Second, it may then be assumed that, at a national level, capital resources would be distributed in favor of agriculture rather than in favor of urbanization and industrialization. It has been argued by Lipton (1977), for example, that a unit of capital invested in agriculture in many countries competes favorably in terms of its income and output effects with one invested in urban industry. The problem with his argument, as is well known, is that it is static. There is remarkably little evidence that investments in agriculture are dynamically more efficient than those in industry. Indeed, as agricultural rates of productivity approach those of industry, as in the most developed countries, their investment requirements approach and often surpass those of industry; after a period of rising returns, they reach diminishing returns again *before* many industries do. Third, the argument in favor of redistributing capital begs the question of where it would come from. In some ways, this is not a pressing problem for the poorest countries of Africa and Asia, who have a long way to go with subsistence or semisubsistence before serious industrialization programs become an issue.[26] But for many countries in Latin America and Asia there is little reason to believe that rural regional development can serve as a replacement for industrialization and urbanization. These countries already have large industrial economies and very high levels of urbanization.

Any successful national development policy, then, must have as a principal goal the establishment of a virtuous circle *between* country and city. This strong emphasis on the development of the rural sector is not a replacement for industrial development, but a complement to it. It is necessary to induce competition for labor between agricultural – rural activities and urban – industrial activities and *thus to reduce the elasticity of urban labor supply*. This implies direct programs for rural development in many countries where rural incomes are low relative to urban incomes. In countries such as Brazil, this would entail agrarian reform to distribute ownership more widely, coupled to reform of the system of agricultural prices and incentives, so as to raise incomes for food producers. The objective of any rural policy must be to create an economy of small and medium sized producers with income levels equivalent, at the very least, to the incomes of workers in the most modern urban industries. Agricultural policy must be coupled to a *rural agricultural income distribution policy* (through distribution of landownership) so as not only to raise the total level of rural income but to distribute it among a large number of people.

[26] Friedmann and Douglass (1978) argue that in these poor countries, capital accumulation would come from selected industrial enclaves. Some would be relatively isolated from the rest of the economy and oriented toward international markets. Others would be semi-autarchic domestic industries, forming 'agropolitan' complexes. The domestic industries might be able to derive their capital from agricultural surplus, if the country is committed to a slow growth path. But it is obvious that the export-oriented enclaves, like those in the contemporary People's Republic of China (PRC), require capital accumulation from elsewhere. The PRC is using foreign investments. One would assume that these industries, in turn, will accumulate capital to modernize the other industries in agropolitan complexes. The stimulus is external.

Regional development policy 2: the global industrial economy and local industrial strategies

8.1 A new context for industrialization

The industrialization strategies of many countries from the 1950s through the late 1970s, in the form of import-substitution and export-promotion policies, were essentially geared toward transferring mass-production industrial systems to the larger and richer Third World countries. The model of mass production is no longer operative over wide segments of the globe, however, and most importantly, the structures of *international* competition which have evolved over the 1970s and 1980s no longer permit its reimplantation. Thus, the basic background conditions for regional industrialization strategies in the 1990s both in developed and in developing economies have been irrevocably altered. Moreover, the paradoxical effect of the new international context for industrialization now taking shape is to make the *local* or 'endogenous' mobilization of resources and skills for industrialization ever more important as a condition of success in the newly internationalized environment. It is under these circumstances that effective regional industrial development policies must now operate.

8.2 The end of Fordism and the rise of a new technological – institutional system

Capitalist production apparatuses may assume many alternative technological and institutional configurations; in the mid-19th century, for example, they were dominated by the classical factory system, whereas in the mid-20th century, mass production prevailed. Each particular configuration consists in a historically determinate technological – institutional model of production comprising a web of production techniques, employment relations, methods of organizing the intrafirm and interfirm divisions of labor, managerial and entrepreneurial relations, and so on. Each such model arises in light of the technological possibilities available at a particular moment in industrial history, in conjunction with the prevailing structure of capitalist competition (that is, an array of market conditions, price structures, factor supplies and prices, and so on).

The 'Fordist' mass-production model was decisively installed in the capitalist economies in the interwar years (Storper and Scott, 1989a). It flourished through a period of high Fordism corresponding more or less to the long postwar boom after which, in the 1970s and especially in the 1980s, it entered into a period of extended crisis, restructuring, and spatial reorganization that is far from over. Fordism was based essentially on mass production, though we should keep in mind that other species of productive activity (such as small-scale batch production and skilled artisanal industry) continued to prosper throughout the Fordist period.

In its classical guise, Fordism was underpinned by large and highly capitalized units of production consisting of either (a) continuous flow processes, as in the case of petrochemicals or steel production, or (b) assembly line processes (and deep technical divisions of labor), as in the cases of cars, electrical appliances, or machinery. Production was geared to an insistent search for internal economies of scale via increasing standardization of outputs, routinization of production processes, and use of rigidly dedicated capital equipment. There was, as a consequence, a tendency both for physical output per plant and for productivity per worker to rise steadily over time. Major plants in leading sectors were, and are, located at the center of networks of upstream producers providing necessary physical inputs and services, sometimes on the basis of non-Fordist artisanal labor processes. As selected production activities within the Fordist system reached technological maturity, they tended to become embodied in branch plants and then to decentralize in search of cheaper labor, first to national and later to international peripheries. It is this type of production that countries such as Brazil and Mexico attempted to install within their borders via policies of import substitution.

By the late 1960s and 1970s, however, the hegemony of this model of industrialization in the advanced capitalist economies was threatened. Internally, market saturation and thoroughgoing spatial decentralization in response to worker militancy were creating high levels of unemployment and productivity slowdowns in the core countries. Externally, competition from Japan and between North America and Western Europe was cutting dramatically into domestic markets in the last two regions. The net result was intensified industrial restructuring and rationalization in the core countries, leading to more plant closures, more decentralization, and greater unemployment. In this context of economic stagnation, declining productivity, and foreign competition, the fiscal bases of Keynesian welfare-statism in the northern hemisphere began to crumble, as was manifested in the prolonged stagflationary crisis of the 1970s. The oil shocks added to these woes.

Initially, the crisis of Fordist mass production in the advanced economies seemed to benefit the industrializing nations of Latin America and Asia, since one of the responses to the crisis on the part of industry was to relocate branch plants to the Third World, in search of lower factor costs. But the downturn in growth rates in the developed world (the deep recession of the early 1980s) interacted with the domestic limitations of this development model in many countries (described in chapter 5) to produce a dramatic stagflationary crisis, with the external debt problem appearing as one of its principal manifestations. By the end of the 1970s, the Fordist model of industrialization and its associated macroeconomic and political arrangements were permanently in disarray in both the northern and the southern hemispheres. Only Japan, which had developed its own alternative pathway to industrialization, escaped the crisis (in part producing the crisis by entering world markets so vigorously on the basis of its alternative model of production).

In the late 1980s, the conditions of capitalist competition are broadly different from what they were two decades ago. In many sectors, there are consistently higher rates of international market cross-penetration, most especially among the advanced countries, and, even though the share of the developed world's markets accounted for by manufactured goods from the Third World has not risen appreciably over this period, the absolute quantities involved—and with them their relative importance to the producing Third World countries—have grown considerably (Gordon, 1988). In short, markets are considerably more contested and contestable over a wide array of goods and services than they were in the heyday of mass production. This condition of market contestation has renewed certain forms of classical capitalist price competition, but more importantly it has also spurred increased nonprice competition in the form of more rapid product differentiation and product changeovers.

In direct contrast to the high levels of market stability, product standardization, and process routinization characteristic of Fordist mass production, the new technological – institutional regime of production now shifting into an increasingly central position in the capitalist economies is based on 'flexibility'. Contemporary flexible production is thus far based on four main groups of industries: (a) selected high-technology industries; (b) craft-based (usually labor-intensive) production in batches; (c) producer and financial services; and (d) restructured consumer durables and production of heavy capital goods. The organizational and locational logics of Fordist mass production are not operative in any of them. Note that the first three of these ensembles, none of which was especially important in the heyday of Fordist mass production, now account for steadily rising shares of employment and output in all the advanced economies, and are gaining ground in several developing economies.

When we speak of flexible production systems we refer to forms of production characterized by a well-developed ability both to shift promptly from one process and/or product configuration to another (dynamic flexibility) and to adjust quantities of output rapidly up or down over the short run without any strongly deleterious effects on levels of efficiency (static flexibility). Both of these types of flexibility are achieved through a variety of intersecting features of the production system. *Within the firm*, flexibility may be attained through the use of general purpose equipment and machinery (that is, not dedicated to one particular output as in mass production but adaptable, often programmable) and/or craft labor processes. *In the domain of interfirm relations*, the principal means of achieving flexibility is the organizational fragmentation of the production process (horizontal and vertical disintegration), creating a deep social division of labor among these firms. This facilitates rapid changeability in the vertical and horizontal combinations of producers in a system.

Subcontracting—in many different institutional guises—is the main form taken by this division of labor, such that the production system often becomes a production network (Piore and Sabel, 1984). These networks are thus within the production process but external to the firm. We may refer to this as the pervasive 'externalization' of production activity in post-Fordism, and note that, as a result of it, the external economies of scale in the production system as a whole are intensified. In addition, the labor markets associated with flexible production systems are typified by high rates of turnover and by the proliferation of part-time and temporary work as well as homework (Angel, 1988; Storper and Scott, 1989b).

As a consequence of these proclivities, individual units of production in flexible production systems are usually less specialized and smaller in size than mass-production units. They are technologically capable of achieving great flexibility of production within their own spheres of operation, and at the same time, this flexibility is multiplied by the system effects of the social division of labor, which permits the formation and reformation of interdependent combinations of producers, as we find in the contemporary textile, electronics, aerospace, and automobile industries. Product differentiation increases as a result, and markets become ever more competitive, as has occurred, for example, in recent years in many market areas in the automobile and clothing industries.

In sum, survival in the capitalist markets of the late 1980s across a wide array of industries is contingent on meeting a number of fundamental and interrelated conditions: (a) High levels of market interpenetration create higher levels of risk for producers, since markets can be more easily contested. (b) Production flexibility is both a response to such risk and its stimulus, since flexibility makes possible more frequent product change-overs—and therefore encourages further market contestation. (c) Flexibility makes possible the production of less standardized goods, but these in turn are oriented toward narrower market niches, thus reducing the scale of production that can be supported in any one country or region; yet the 'background' investments in equipment, product planning, and marketing are, if anything, greater than ever, especially in technology-intensive production processes or design-intensive products. These investments require amortization either over a large quantity of output of one good, or over a large range of differentiated goods. (d) All these conditions make it unlikely that specialized products will find their markets exclusively within the borders of one country, even the largest and wealthiest, and so require increasingly that products be geared both toward domestic and toward international markets and hence toward meeting international standards of price, design, and quality. The implication of this for industrial policy is straightforward: promoting the growth of sectors producing tradeable goods is the key to increasing the level of production within a region. To the extent that tradeable production within a region is expanded, local employment both in tradeable and in nontradeable sectors can expand.

The critical constraint on expansion of nontradeable sector employment is the level of production of tradeable goods and services.

There are additional historical conditions specific to the Third World which define the possibilities for successful industrialization strategies there. High levels of external debt, for one, require that countries increase their levels of exports in order to earn foreign exchange credits with which to service such debt and so that they may continue to purchase foreign goods such as industrial inputs. More importantly, even in the absence of high levels of debt, exportation has proven to be an important development strategy, as realized in the relative successess of several Asian countries (see Evans, 1987). Export-oriented industrialization permits enlargement of the productive forces at a greater rate than would be provided by enlargement of domestic markets alone (even assuming that the state of class relations were such as to permit growth in the domestic market) so long as exports are not contingent upon keeping domestic labor cheap to the point that the domestic market is depressed to a greater extent than is compensated by the volume of exports. It is, of course, in coordinating these two rates—expansion of exports and wage-induced growth of the domestic market—that the principal task of industrialization policy as a whole lies. In today's market conditions, that coordination can only come through a deft combination of continual improvement in the price–performance ratios of a country's products, that is, through improvements in quality which in turn permit increases in prices and thus the growth of domestic wages; and both of these must be underpinned by regular increases in factor productivity. Note, too, that continually changing the price-performance characteristics of the product has its analog in the technological character of the production process: being equipped to make frequent changes in the product implies an ability to adapt process technologies incrementally, which in turn should permit their adaptation to local factor-market conditions. In other words, technological competence is no longer a question of importing 'inappropriate' technologies, but one of *making such technologies appropriate* by mastering the ability to adapt them more or less continuously on a number of fronts. This is what the Japanese did in the 1950s as they developed the now-famous Toyota 'flexible' production system: they adapted imported US equipment to the more demanding conditions of the Japanese environment, with its then-small internal markets, capital scarcities, and relatively labor-rich conditions (Cusumano, 1985).

The specific context of the newly industrializing countries of Latin America, which is discussed above, constrains their industrialization strategies in ways which are broadly convergent with the conditions faced by the advanced economies in adapting to the new technological–institutional regime of flexible industrialization: (a) they must be, to an increasing degree, oriented toward exportation; (b) they must seek product differentiation and specialization (not only because of the vagaries of world markets and their increasingly specialized market structures, but also because of Third World nations' own needs to move up the price-performance curve); and (c) by virtue of the last two conditions, static and dynamic production process flexibility are both now indispensable.

8.3 Post-Fordist development: 'endogenous' but externally oriented?

Industrialization policies addressed to the realities of the new techno-logical-institutional system may present a major opportunity for Third World industrial powers. The fundamental contestability of many markets—in both price and nonprice terms—implies a greater turnover of 'openings' in the markets of the capitalist world as a whole. This does not mean that there is indefinite capacity for exportation on the part of all countries (something which is mathematically impossible), but that the structure of market niches is more fluid than it once was. Thus, in principle, Third World nations who develop production apparatuses that are both quantitatively and qualitatively flexible and underpinned by effective sectoral strategies, do enjoy the possibility of occupying new market niches and thereby changing the composition of their industrial output significantly. Moreover, as Schmitz (1988) points out, many Third World economies have for a long time had dense tissues of structurally heterogenous small and medium sized firms for reasons of necessity, that is, as a means of coping with pervasive economic uncertainty and scarce resources. The opportunity now exists, at least in principle, to turn what has for the most part been viewed by social scientists and economic planners as a sign of backwardness and disadvantage, into an asset. But, as we shall now see, the process of adaptation is neither cheap nor easy.

Development strategies for post-Fordist industrialization are, by necessity, different from those intended to implant Fordist forms of production. Fordist mass production was characterized, above all, by the possibility of separating conception—in the sense of design of products and processes and planning of production—from execution, or the actual activity of taking inputs and transforming them into final outputs. By the end of the 1960s, this separation had become widespread in mass-production systems in three respects. First, there was considerable deskilling of production workers so that they were reduced to carrying out tasks in endless repetition with little connection to any kind of decisionmaking, a condition made possible by the technical division of labor and its accompanying routinization of tasks (Lipietz, 1977; Walker and Storper, 1981). Although the appellation 'semiskilled' was given to the industrial worker, in reality large proportions of the workers in Fordist factories possessed few specialized skills at all, and most could be trained in a matter of hours or a few days at most. Second, many phases of the production system were isolated from conception because product standardization and process routinization made possible high levels of mechanization using dedicated (that is, specialized and quasi-automatic) capital equipment.

This state of so-called 'technological maturity' meant that considerable parts of the Fordist production system were reduced to 'turnkey' operations that could be duplicated in any place possessing urban infrastructure and a labor force of sufficient size. By the early 1970s, the separation of production activity from conception activity had proceeded far up the input chain to many components. Third, as a correlate of these latter points, spatial separation of execution from conception activities was increasingly well developed with the maturity of the system. In the early postwar decades, branch plants were relocated from the core production regions of the advanced nations to their own peripheral regions, such as the US South. But later on, large segments of the upstream input chain became relocatable as well. For example, by the time Brazil entered its industrial boom in the 1970s, it was technologically not difficult to locate very large portions of the Fordist production system far from the developed countries where much of the conception activity continued to take place (Fröbel et al, 1980). Import-substitution industrialization policies were, in effect, convergent with the organizational and locational logic of Fordist mass production at the global level.

Some aspects of the pervasive separation of conception from execution characteristic of mass production break down in flexible production. First, dynamic flexibility rests on the proper mobilization and organization of networks of producers. The flexible interfirm division of labor defines some of the possibilities for product and process innovations. Given the practical problems and questions constantly generated by interaction between different producers, informal processes of technical innovation and change are set into motion. To take an example from the developed world, much innovation in specialized tile equipment in the Sassuolo district of central Italy has been stimulated by interactions between tile producers (with their needs) and equipment producers (with their specialized capabilities) (Russo, 1985). As a result of these interfirm interactions, Sassuolo has become not only a leading tile producer, but a prominent exporter of tile-producing equipment as well. At a smaller scale, the same seems to be true of textile producers and equipment makers in Blumenau and Joinvile in the state of Santa Catarina in Brazil, or the shoemakers of Novo Hamburgo in Rio Grande do Sul (see footnote 13). In the process of carrying out business through flexible production networks, entrepreneurs learn about the manifold facets of production in the industrial complex. The result is the formation of a local business culture in which practical forms of knowledge about production processes and markets are socialized, and tastes and sensibilities about materials and product designs are finely honed. In some cases, the socialization of useful knowledge may be carried further by the public provision of educational infrastructure serving the local complex. Looked at this way, the production system is no longer a firm, but instead a wider socioeconomic organization which creates and defines entrepreneurial opportunities (Bellandi, 1986).

Second, the organizational nature of the flexible production system creates potential problems of economic and social coordination which can only be resolved through the creation of appropriate local institutions and social practices. Flexible production systems represent collectivities of interdependent producers whose transactional relations may in part be mediated by market mechanisms and individual decisionmaking behavior, that is, buying and selling relations. But markets alone rarely resolve the problems of flexibility stemming from the interdependence that comes with the division of labor between firms, on the one hand, accompanied by the multiplication of *in*dependent decisionmaking centers on the other. Thus, in successful flexible production systems, mechanisms of formal coordination—such as contracts and strategic alliances—or new types of organizations which are specialized in system coordination—such as the Japanese *Keiretsu* or the Italian *impannatori*—may come into being. They are often strongly tied to the regional base of the production system and supported in many cases by public policies (Bianchi et al, 1988).

Another route to system coordination is the emergence of informal relations of trust, where the producers in an industrial community learn over time about the behavior, idiosyncrasies, and capabilities of other entrepreneurs. Trust, however, as a foundation of economic relations, is a 'double-edged sword': it can retard economic development where it is a strictly *private* form of transactional coordination, as in the case of mafias and aristocracies, for these, by definition, restrict entry of new producers; where trust is highly generalized and public, on the other hand, it serves to sustain transactions and reduce the costs for established producers, while at the same time allowing new entrants into the community (Gambetta, 1988). Informal systems of trust and formal coordinating agencies both serve to increase the flow of information throughout the production system and so encourage the dynamic of innovation referred to above. The point is that the management of flexible forces of production depends, to an increasing extent, on the generalization of appropriate social relations, *at the level of the production system itself*.

That these externalized mechanisms and habits of coordination are frequently lacking in Third World economies is well known. Hirschman (1965), for example, cites the problem of many Third World airline companies: they are as modern as any other company once in the air (once the machinery starts moving), but on the ground the situation is often very different. Many of the growth-pole theorists failed to understand that introduction of modern technology alone would not automatically induce the establishment of comparable technologies or social relations upstream or downstream. Nonetheless, at least under Fordism large-scale modern technological 'islands' could be implanted in social formations with otherwise incompatible social relations, however dramatic were the occasional breakdowns in servicing and maintaining these technological systems. The resulting industrial structure was necessarily highly oligopolistic as a consequence of the widespread internalization of functions (within the large firm) that could not be trusted to the external transactional environment. This form of large-scale market failure does not, however, appear to be compatible with successful flexible production, for it is precisely in the structure of interfirm relations that much static and dynamic flexibility lie.

Third, the labor skills required to carry out flexible production are different in many ways from those involved in mass production (Storper and Scott, 1989b). To be sure, certain phases of flexible production systems continue to depend on extremely deskilled and highly exploited labor (particularly at lower tiers of the subcontracting system). Nevertheless, it appears also that the ratio of deskilled to reskilled labor is lower in the typical flexible production system than it was in the Fordist mass-production system. There are higher proportions of entrepreneurs, technicians, product designers, system coordinators, and so on; in addition, much flexibility is necessarily carried out through the redeployability of labor on the shop floor, in the form of work teams and broader job categories. Internal work flexibility generally requires more polyvalent skills than did the performance of work under Fordist conditions, and much of this human capital is firm-specific, since it requires flexible interaction within the firm around a changing mix of production tasks and projects. Although these conditions may describe a minority of the workforce in the flexible production system, it is nonetheless a minority sizable enough to require much more careful attention to the creation and reproduction of labor skills than was the case in Fordist mass production (as witnessed in the current worries about the educational systems in such countries as the United States and France). Flexible production, then, cannot be transferred willy-nilly to uneducated and unskilled Third World labor forces; it requires the development of considerable production skills, which are produced via both formal education and practical experience in the local labor market. Such skill development, however, may not be compatible with the high levels of workforce entry and exit observed in many Brazilian industrial centers, where workers migrate in and then, after one of their frequent layoffs, return to their region of origin or migrate to yet another region in search of employment.

Flexible production imposes new requirements (and to be sure, new difficulties) on those places wishing to industrialize, for it requires the endogenous mobilization and sustenance of resources (for example, labor) and the nurturing of complex social relations (trust, entrepreneurship). Paradoxically, it seems that to serve global markets one must now mobilize local resources and skills to a greater extent than ever before, in order to master the conception that is crucial to successful execution of flexible production. This paradox was apparently understood early on by the Japanese and is now being taken very seriously in Korea and Singapore, as they attempt to propel themselves into the ranks of globally effective industrial powers. It should be evident that this form of industrialization is not cheap or simple to develop. There is no way to legislate the flexible production system into existence simply by imposing market barriers, as Brazil has attempted to do with respect to the computer industry. Taken alone, the latter type of policy can at the most insure that products developed elsewhere are copied and produced for the domestic market (usually at much higher prices), while not leading to the dynamic product innovations that could permit exportation nor to the process innovations that would permit price reductions and enlargement of domestic markets. The creation of skills, mobilization of social resources, and identification of feasible and unoccupied market niches, all involve long-term and large-scale investments of social time and resources, with high risks of failure and long maturity and amortization periods.

8.4 Post-Fordism, urbanization, and regional development in the Third World
All of the flexible production industries, as noted, are marked by networks of specialized producers, in which small and medium sized firms are heavily represented. The firms in these systems tend to have dense transactional relations. Many of these transactions are potentially very costly to carry out, for they involve precise delivery times, constant renegotiation of inputs and outputs, and development and exchange of idiosyncratic and changing information. Firms in flexible production industries therefore have a tendency to concentrate geographically in order to reduce the costs and difficulties of carrying out such transactions and in order to maximize their access to the cultural and informational context of the production system. Production flexibility and readjustment are further encouraged by the geographical pooling of labor demands and supplies; this facilitates accelerated turnover, reduces the costs of labor-market search both for employers and for workers, allows the process of social-ization and training to occur with greatest ease, and thus promotes the matching of workers to tasks. Accordingly, the turn toward production flexibility in the developed countries has been marked by a decisive geographical reconcentration of production and the resurgence of the phenomenon of the industrial district; likewise, the emergence of flexible production has belied predictions (common in the 1970s) of the demise of locationally dense production systems.[27] In the developed countries, for example, we see major reconcentrations of business and commercial service activity in New York, London, Tokyo, and other 'world cities', together with dependent clusters in parts of their suburban fringe areas; revitalized craft-based industry is currently most highly developed in the specialized clusters of the Third Italy, but can also be found in France, Denmark, the United States, and Germany; new high-technology industrial districts are found at such locations as Silicon Valley and Orange County

[27] These districts are, of course, not self-contained but are situated within wider and expanding regional, national, and international divisions of labor.

in California, in the Scientific City south of Paris, in Dallas–Fort Worth, and in the Cambridge–Reading–Bristol axis in England; and flexibly restructured production of consumer durables, which is most highly developed in Japan, takes such form as the dense Toyota City production complex (Scott, 1988b). In Brazil, incipient flexible production zones have appeared in the textile and machinery industries of the small cities of Santa Catarina such as Blumenau and along the Valley of Itajaí, as well as in a number of cities in Rio Grande do Sul and in the western part of the state of São Paulo; moreover, Brazil is attempting to develop a high-technology industrial district in Campinas, located about 100 km outside of the city of São Paulo.

The development of flexible production represents both a danger and an opportunity for regional policy in industrializing nations. On the one hand, there is no process of steady decentralization of production from the developed world to the underdeveloped world on which industrializing countries can rely for their future; the geographical reconcentration of production means that the locations of growth centers are increasingly in the developed world itself, as is evident from the examples provided above. On the other hand, successful industrialization policies addressed to the realities of the new technological–institutional system present the opportunity, in some cases, to break with patterns of extreme metropolitan primacy. Flexible production sectors are typically relatively independent of the particular kinds of agglomeration economies available in old centers of Fordist industry, that is, linkage into mass-production complexes and access to their attendant labor skills. It is for this reason that so many of the flexible production industries in the developed world have grown at locations far removed from the traditional industrial heartlands of those countries (the Sunbelt of the USA, the Southeast of England, the South of France). It is perhaps also for this reason that the incipient examples of flexible production in Brazil are all well outside the orbit of metropolitan São Paulo. In the case of the industries of Santa Catarina for example, it appears that the predecessors of present-day firms had detailed vertical and horizontal linkages in the community and that today's successful firms have strong connections to local subcontractors and specialized equipment suppliers, as well as very specific and traditional connections to local labor markets (personal communication, 1986: Kipnis, 1983). The opening up of the 'window of locational opportunity' by the appearance of new sectors and new production methods thus offers the possibility of reducing the spatial concentration of industry.

Still, even in the developed countries there is no known successful policy formula for creating or sustaining such flexible production complexes. An enormous academic literature on such things as 'technopolis' policies, 'creative' regions, and so on exists purporting to identify the keys to replicating flexible production systems in new places. But this literature is largely devoid of specific analytical content, since for the most part it relies on ad hoc descriptions of the characteristics of growing industrial regions (for example, that they have large numbers of engineers and scientists, a 'high quality of life', or a 'good business climate'). The cloth of these lists can be cut to fit virtually any situation (Scott and Storper, 1987). The danger is that those simplistic policy formulas will be handed down to Third World countries by analysts whose views are largely misplaced even for the developed countries.

Likewise, although the analysis here might appear to lead to policies which emphasize 'small and medium sized enterprises' and 'growth poles', there are fundamental differences with the conventional connotations of these terms. First, the emphasis of policy must be not on strengthening the small firm per se, as is the wont in much of the literature, but on firms of different sizes and functions in relation to a *system of firms embedded in a production process*. Second, whereas conventional growth-pole strategies started from the final output firm, and expected upstream input producers to come into existence and to locate near the final output unit, a reinvigorated local industrial policy would have to place great importance on the development of the social division of labor and specialized labor markets 'from the bottom up'. Thus, we can surely reformulate the notion of a growth-pole policy in an era of flexible production as consisting of measures designed: (a) to foster the intricate interrelations between firms, as described above; (b) to promote and sustain the coordination of these same relations through both formal and informal methods, including the identification of appropriate markets; (c) to further the creation of local labor skills and the operation of the local labor market; and (d) to carry out appropriate processes of local social regulation, including the development of communities of trust (Storper and Scott, 1989).

Such policies are hardly the stuff of traditional regional development or urban planning policy apparatuses, for they can consist neither simply of elaborate financial incentives (as in the case, for example, of Brazil's SUDENE) nor of regulations (as in much industrial and regional policy). Neither of these approaches can carry out the necessary task of building up flexible production as a system of social relations and transactions through the steady accumulation of local knowledge and development of local social practice as well as investment of capital.

The type of development process which would follow from successful post-Fordist industrialization policies is likely to be extremely spatially selective: flexible production systems create highly concentrated growth centers and some places benefit while others are left behind. There is no suggestion here that the contemporary development of new industrial spaces leads toward the final interregional equilibrium, though it does offer the logical possibility of reducing polarization through the multiplication of territorial growth centers, or what I have termed 'polarization reversal by repolarization'. It will be necessary to find out much more about the technological and organizational characteristics of the successful complexes which are outside the major poles; and then to investigate the political and economic conditions of the region that give rise to these complexes and nurture them (Becattini, 1987; Sforzi, 1988).

This directly implies that *selective* secondary city development, in *concert* with sectoral policies, will be more effective than any blanket policy of discriminating against large cities to the benefit of smaller ones (see Rondinelli, 1977). If the São Paulo experience is any guide, these policies would have to emphasize linkage between different industrial complexes, including both small and large cities if necessary, as well as 'horizontal' linkages between small cities; in other words, the full complexity of growth-transmission linkages must be taken into account (Pred, 1977). No urbanization policy based simply on an idealized urban system geometry, ignorant of the endogenous dynamics of production complexes and their very complex spatial structure, is likely to succeed.

A whole new approach to the industrial complex is needed to carry out these tasks successfully: one which stays true to the notion of development as a series of disequilibrium states realized 'from the bottom up' through a changing division of labor. It is through such processes that comparative advantages are built-up or *created* in a locality through the accumulation of capital, skill, and organizational capacities and structures.

9

Conclusion

By way of conclusion, I would like simply to underscore the methodological agenda of this book briefly. I have attempted here to use tools from a number of fields, including industrial location theory, regional development theory, and economic development theory. I have attempted to enrich them by emphasizing the division of labor and the organization of production systems. I have, moreover, stressed the relations between industrial and regional microeconomics and macroeconomic dynamics. It is a tall methodological agenda and, no doubt, there are many weaknesses and problems, but it remains, I believe the only direction in which successful regional development analysis can go.

It should be obvious that the kind of theory proposed here, while gaining in explanatory power and appreciation of dynamics, makes no pretense to the prediction of particular locational patterns or patterns of urban development. But in my view, the loss of 'predictive power' or 'precision' is more ostensible than real, since conventional models can only make ceteris paribus predictions or measurements ex post, and manifestly cannot penetrate urban, regional, or industrial *dynamics* nor their *causes*.

I have drawn on this analysis to suggest that any economic policy (that is, import substitution, etc), like any discrete regional or spatial policy, which lacks the analytical perspective of political economy, is simply a futile and utopian practice. Locating forces of production in a region without changing social relations is exactly such a type of futile policy.

The whole point of attempting this new integration between location theory, urban and regional economics, and the theory of economic development generally is not to depreciate the importance of regional policy, but to reawaken our sense of its possibilities, and especially of using local and regional development strategies as central components not only in local development, but in national development as well. This goes well beyond the simple 'use' of the locality for nonlocal goals; it involves a new kind of relationship between local, endogenous dynamics and the broader goals of the national society.

Appendix A

Table A.1. Spatial concentration (%) of manufacturing employment, 1970-75 (source: Storper, 1984; IBGE, 1970; 1980).

	GSP/State [a]		GSP/Brazil [a]		State/Brazil [a]	
	1970	1975	1970	1975	1970	1975
Traditional						
Textiles	62	57	34	30	54	53
Clothing, shoes	69	69	33	29	48	43
Food	40	43	13	12	31	29
Beverages	34	26	11	8	33	39
Printing	84	80	36	34	43	43
Furniture	69	65	29	28	42	43
Leather	38	35	11	9	28	26
Dynamic A						
Nonmetals [b]	55	52	22	20	41	37
Metallurgy	83	80	46	45	56	57
Paper	73	73	42	41	57	56
Rubber	79	75	57	53	72	70
Chemicals	59	64	32	33	55	52
Pharmaceuticals	95	90	58	50	67	55
Dynamic B						
Machinery	72	68	44	41	61	61
Electrical	89	84	66	60	74	72
Transport	86	78	64	49	75	64
Plastics	92	88	65	56	70	64
Overall						
Traditional	57.9	57.9	25.0	25.1	43.2	43.4
Dynamic A	71.6	71.2	37.2	36.0	51.9	50.6
Dynamic B	82.5	75.5	57.1	48.4	69.2	64.1
All industry	69.1	67.9	35.4	34.8	51.2	51.2

[a] State is state of São Paulo; GSP Greater São Paulo.
[b] Nonmetallic minerals.

Table A.2. Shift-share analysis (N national share, M industrial shift, C competitive shift) of industrial employment for selected states, 1970–80 (source: IBGE, 1970; 1980).

	São Paulo					Minas Gerais					Rio-Guarabara				
	N (82.7%)	M		C		N (82.7%)	M		C		N (82.7%)	M		C	
	no.	no.	%	no.	%	no.	no.	%	no.	%	no.	no.	%	no.	%
Traditional	407885	-107887	-21.9	-71808	-14.6	77180	-20414	-21.9	1130	1.2	139639	-36935	-21.9	-78736	-46.6
Textiles	153238	-134449	-72.6	-17595	-9.5	26825	-23536	-72.6	-813	-2.5	35282	-30956	-72.6	-12869	-30.2
Clothing, shoes	65027	76155	96.8	-24062	-30.6	5793	6785	96.8	10418	148.7	20843	24409	96.8	-21201	-84.1
Food	96582	-18280	-15.7	-16307	-14.0	27089	-5127	-15.7	1004	3.1	38140	-7219	-15.7	-19047	-41.3
Beverages	15904	-15939	-82.9	-2029	-10.5	3782	-3791	-82.9	1322	28.9	8789	-8808	-82.9	-3050	-28.7
Printing	34444	-15141	-36.4	3583	8.6	5376	-2363	-36.4	-348	-5.3	20662	-9083	-36.4	-11624	-46.5
Furniture	36464	-7423	-16.8	-6318	-14.3	6368	-1296	-16.8	248	3.2	13304	-2708	-16.8	-11708	-72.8
Leather	6226	-1706	-22.7	-182	-2.4	1946	-533	-22.7	-1255	-53.3	2619	-717	-22.7	-1089	-34.4
Dynamic A	316882	-9771	-2.5	-51812	-13.5	52389	-1615	-2.5	23691	37.4	74516	-2298	-2.5	-36579	-40.6
Nonmetals	79296	2160	2.3	-35361	-36.9	17863	487	2.3	12024	55.7	22527	614	2.3	-17997	-66.1
Metallurgy	123160	24591	16.5	3842	2.6	28102	5611	16.5	1043	3.1	28540	5698	16.5	-18672	-54.1
Paper	31790	-8585	-22.3	-2828	-7.4	2124	-573	-22.3	164	6.4	7308	-1974	-22.3	-1226	-13.9
Rubber	19648	-2575	-10.8	-3048	-12.8	748	-98	-10.8	1012	112.0	1991	-261	-10.8	-978	-40.6
Chemicals	47530	-15114	-26.3	-9543	-16.6	2998	-953	-26.3	3330	91.9	14149	-4499	-26.3	-8533	-49.9
Pharmaceuticals	15458	-13512	-72.3	-1610	-8.6	555	-485	-72.3	514	76.6	*	*	*	*	*
Dynamic B	284212	189634	55.2	-80314	-23.4	16916	11287	55.2	25430	124.3	55280	36884	55.2	-39814	-59.6
Machinery	90793	126886	115.6	-3278	-3.0	11635	16260	115.6	1091	7.8	22159	30968	115.6	-29732	-111.0
Electrical	71019	24179	28.2	-16044	-18.7	2550	868	28.2	1670	54.1	12048	4102	28.2	-12070	-82.8
Transport	97684	-5965	-5.0	-37084	-31.4	2392	-146	-5.0	14566	503.6	16094	-983	-5.0	2894	14.9
Plastics	24715	28850	96.5	-8223	-27.5	339	396	96.5	2010	490.3	4978	5811	96.5	-3920	-65.1
Total	1008979	71976	5.9	-203934	-16.7	146485	-10742	-6.1	50249	28.4	269435	-2349	-0.7	-155129	-47.6

Table A.2 (continued)

	Paraná					Santa Catarina					Rio Grande do Sul				
	N (82.7%)	M no.	M %	C no.	C %	N (82.7%)	M no.	M %	C no.	C %	N (82.7%)	M no.	M %	C no.	C %
Traditional	31 313	−8 282	−21.9	16 177	42.7	38 753	−10 250	−21.9	36 540	78.0	94 178	−24 910	−21.9	50 269	44.1
Textiles	3 598	−3 157	−72.6	2 395	55.0	18 135	−15 912	−72.6	10 798	49.2	8 007	−7 025	−72.6	4 508	46.6
Clothing, shoes	1 206	1 413	96.8	3 541	242.7	2 260	2 647	96.8	21 309	779.7	28 111	32 922	96.8	−3 215	−9.5
Food	14 463	−2 737	−15.7	4 808	27.5	10 504	−1 988	−15.7	6 104	48.1	33 002	−6 246	−15.7	−6 361	15.9
Beverages	1 904	−1 908	−82.9	429	18.6	967	−969	−82.9	537	45.9	5 398	−5 410	−82.9	916	14.0
Printing	3 138	−1 380	−36.4	854	22.5	1 060	−466	−36.4	1 253	97.7	5 406	−2 377	−36.4	−114	−1.7
Furniture	6 018	−1 225	−16.8	4 995	68.6	5 224	−1 063	−16.8	4 424	70.0	7 785	−1 585	−16.8	5 662	60.1
Leather	986	−270	−22.7	137	11.5	603	−165	−22.7	−219	−30.0	6 468	−1 772	−22.7	2 734	35.0
Dynamic A	22 171	−684	−2.5	8 041	30.0	18 526	−571	−2.5	15 424	68.8	43 056	−1 328	−2.5	4 214	8.1
Nonmetals	10 315	281	2.3	2 434	19.5	8 148	222	2.3	9 639	97.8	11 487	313	2.3	913	6.6
Metallurgy	3 614	722	16.5	3 163	72.4	4 336	866	16.5	6 063	115.6	19 656	3 925	16.5	−2 955	−12.4
Paper	4 318	−1 166	−22.3	−135	−2.6	4 126	−1 114	−22.3	−1 226	−24.6	3 463	−935	−22.3	1 328	31.7
Rubber	563	−74	−10.8	459	67.4	244	−32	−10.8	273	92.6	2 107	−276	−10.8	732	28.7
Chemicals	3 360	−1 068	−26.3	2 459	60.5	1 674	−532	−26.3	411	20.3	5 745	−1 827	−26.3	1 495	21.5
Pharmaceuticals	*	*	*	*	*	*	*	*	*	*	599	−523	−72.3	697	96.2
Dynamic B	6 633	4 426	55.2	17 022	212.2	9 348	6 237	55.2	9 676	85.6	23 172	15 461	55.2	16 498	58.9
Machinery	2 909	4 066	115.6	7 216	205.1	4 840	6 764	115.6	2 952	50.4	11 714	16 371	115.6	1 322	9.3
Electrical	713	243	28.2	3 793	440.0	783	267	28.2	3 172	335.0	4 078	1 388	28.2	1 962	39.8
Transport	2 095	−128	−5.0	4 168	164.6	1 709	−104	−5.0	1 183	57.2	6 347	−388	−5.0	7 353	95.8
Plastics	916	1 070	96.5	1 020	92.1	2 015	2 352	96.5	−674	−27.6	1 034	1 207	96.5	2 744	219.5
Total	60 116	−4 540	−6.2	41 240	56.7	66 627	−4 584	−5.7	61 640	76.5	160 406	−10 777	−5.6	70 981	36.6

* Data not available.

Appendix B

Basic data on Brazilian industry used as basis for figures and tables

Table B.1. Sectoral composition (number of workers) of manufacturing employment, Brazil and selected states (source: IBGE, 1970; 1980).

	Brazil			São Paulo			Minas Gerais			Rio-Guanabara		
	1970	1980	1970–80 (%)	1970	1980	1970–80 (%)	1970	1980	1970–80 (%)	1970	1980	1970–80 (%)
Traditional	1167172	1877043	60.82	493257	721447	46.26	93334	151229	62.03	168866	192834	14.19
Textiles	342839	377600	10.14	185312	186506	0.64	32440	34916	7.63	42667	34124	−20.02
Clothing, shoes	164512	459869	179.54	78637	195756	148.94	7006	30002	328.23	25205	49256	95.42
Food	372401	622062	67.04	116797	178792	53.08	32759	55725	70.11	46123	57997	25.74
Beverages	58619	58512	−0.18	19233	17169	−10.73	4574	5888	28.73	10628	7559	−28.88
Printing	97087	142078	46.34	41653	64538	54.94	6501	9166	40.99	24987	24942	−0.18
Furniture	105322	174685	65.86	44096	66819	51.53	7701	13021	69.08	16089	14977	−6.91
Leather	26392	42237	60.04	7529	11867	57.62	2353	2511	6.71	3167	3979	25.64
Dynamic A	738459	1330278	80.14	383207	628506	66.62	63354	137818	117.54	90112	125751	39.55
Nonmetals	236506	437405	84.94	95893	141988	48.07	21602	51976	140.61	27242	32386	18.88
Metallurgy	266926	531729	99.20	148938	300531	101.78	33984	68740	102.27	34513	50079	45.10
Paper	66994	107433	60.36	38444	58822	53.01	2568	4282	66.74	8838	12947	46.49
Rubber	32863	56476	71.85	23760	37784	59.02	904	2566	183.95	2408	3160	31.23
Chemicals	104367	163227	56.40	57478	80351	39.79	3625	8999	148.25	17111	18228	6.53
Pharmaceuticals	30801	34008	10.41	18694	19030	1.80	671	1255	87.03	*	8951	*
Dynamic B	496818	1181764	137.87	343699	937231	114.50	20457	74090	262.17	66850	119200	78.31
Machinery	180431	538146	198.26	109797	324198	195.27	14070	43056	206.01	26797	50192	87.30
Electrical	115485	243494	110.84	85884	165038	92.16	3084	8172	164.98	14570	18650	28.00
Transport	158336	281272	77.64	118130	178765	46.25	2893	19707	581.20	19463	37469	92.51
Plastics	42566	118852	179.22	29883	75230	151.71	410	3155	669.51	6020	12889	114.10
Total	2402449	4329085	82.69	1220163	2097184	71.88	177145	363137	104.99	325828	437785	34.36
Others	232191	529124	127.89	68914	181194	162.93	9210	25285	174.54	31205	38611	23.73
Total all industry	2634650	4918209	86.68	1289077	2278378	76.74	186355	388422	108.43	357033	476396	33.43

Table B.1 (continued)

	Paraná			Santa Catarina			Rio Grande do Sul			Goias		
	1970	1980	1970–80 (%)	1970	1980	1970–80 (%)	1970	1980	1970–80 (%)	1970	1980	1970–80 (%)
Traditional	37 867	77 075	103.54	46 864	111 907	138.78	113 890	233 427	104.96	11 406	24 862	117.97
Textiles	4 351	7 187	65.18	21 931	34 953	59.33	9 683	15 173	56.70	833	1 190	42.86
Clothing, shoes	1 459	7 619	422.21	2 733	28 949	959.24	33 995	91 813	170.08	891	2 415	171.04
Food	17 490	34 023	94.53	12 703	27 323	115.09	39 909	73 025	82.98	7 323	15 614	113.22
Beverages	2 302	2 727	18.46	1 169	1 704	45.77	6 528	7 432	13.85	415	886	113.49
Printing	3 795	6 408	68.85	1 282	3 129	144.07	6 538	9 454	44.60	733	2 034	177.49
Furniture	7 278	17 066	134.49	6 317	14 901	135.09	9 415	21 278	126.00	1 037	2 468	137.99
Leather	1 192	2 045	71.56	729	948	30.04	7 822	15 252	94.99	174	255	46.55
Dynamic A	26 811	56 339	110.13	22 404	55 783	148.99	52 068	98 011	88.24	4 531	17 737	291.46
Nonmetals	12 474	25 504	104.46	9 853	27 862	182.78	13 891	26 604	91.52	3 390	12 523	269.41
Metallurgy	4 371	11 870	171.56	5 243	16 507	214.84	23 770	44 396	86.77	643	3 518	447.12
Paper	5 222	8 239	57.77	4 989	6 774	35.78	4 188	8 044	92.07	96	242	152.08
Rubber	681	1 629	139.21	295	780	164.41	2 548	5 111	100.59	270	356	31.85
Chemicals	4 063	8 813	116.91	2 024	3 576	76.68	6 947	12 360	77.92	78	596	664.10
Pharmaceuticals	*	284	*	*	284	*	724	1 496	106.63	54	502	829.63
Dynamic B	8 021	36 101	350.08	11 304	36 564	223.46	28 022	83 153	196.74	899	3 725	314.35
Machinery	3 518	17 709	403.38	5 853	20 409	248.69	14 166	43 573	207.59	463	1 522	228.73
Electrical	862	5 610	550.81	947	5 169	445.83	4 931	12 359	150.64	189	796	321.16
Transport	2 533	8 668	242.20	2 067	4 855	134.88	7 675	20 987	173.45	247	1 149	365.18
Plastics	1 108	4 114	271.30	2 437	6 131	151.58	1 250	6 234	398.72	*	258	*
Total	72 699	169 515	133.17	80 572	204 254	153.50	193 980	414 591	113.73	16 836	46 324	175.15
Others	39 275	62 363	58.79	32 703	62 597	91.41	23 573	41 757	77.14	1 768	7 002	296.04
Total all industry	111 974	231 878	107.08	113 275	266 851	135.58	217 553	456 348	109.76	18 604	53 326	186.64

* Data not available.

Table B.2. Sectoral composition (number of plants) of manufacturing plants, Brazil and selected states (source: IBGE, 1970; 1980).

	Brazil			São Paulo			Minas Gerais			Rio-Guanabara		
	1970	1980	1970–80 (%)	1970	1980	1970–80 (%)	1970	1980	1970–80 (%)	1970	1980	1970–80 (%)
Traditional	86 321	96 321	11.72	25 651	27 757	8.21	10 052	10 782	7.26	7 783	8 003	2.83
Textiles	5 309	6 062	14.18	3 251	3 194	−1.75	294	469	59.52	330	329	−0.30
Clothing, shoes	8 613	15 338	78.08	4 087	6 747	65.08	721	1 486	106.10	982	1 581	61.00
Food	46 815	49 366	5.45	11 102	10 540	−5.06	5 900	5 664	−4.00	4 022	3 781	−5.99
Beverages	4 798	2 925	−39.04	1 025	575	−43.90	906	777	−14.24	269	145	−46.10
Printing	5 526	8 328	50.71	2 185	3 263	49.34	551	852	54.63	1 005	1 124	11.84
Furniture	13 127	12 667	−3.50	3 596	3 081	−14.32	1 412	1 342	−4.96	1 118	1 002	−10.38
Leather	2 032	1 635	−19.54	405	357	−11.85	268	192	−28.36	57	41	−28.07
Dynamic A	40 367	64 465	59.70	13 250	17 579	32.67	4 202	8 197	95.07	3 040	3 549	16.74
Nonmetals	25 367	43 170	70.18	6 569	8 147	24.02	2 854	6 196	117.10	1 042	1 348	29.37
Metallurgy	9 631	14 407	48.82	4 389	6 251	42.42	972	1 499	54.22	1 290	1 432	11.01
Paper	1 178	1 704	44.65	618	892	44.34	69	89	28.99	162	216	33.33
Rubber	974	1 273	30.70	398	514	29.15	93	147	58.06	79	83	5.06
Chemicals	2 645	3 419	29.26	1 069	1 553	45.28	167	220	31.74	308	366	18.83
Pharmaceuticals	522	492	−5.75	207	222	7.25	47	46	−2.13	159	104	−34.59
Dynamic B	14 529	19 719	35.72	7 103	10 851	52.77	942	1 242	31.85	1 627	1 690	3.87
Machinery	6 744	9 748	44.54	3 185	5 516	73.19	517	664	28.43	738	699	−5.28
Electrical	3 155	3 337	5.77	1 630	2 110	29.45	240	200	−16.67	424	350	−17.45
Transport	3 319	3 983	20.01	1 389	1 504	8.28	157	279	77.71	286	374	30.77
Plastics	1 311	2 651	102.21	899	1 721	91.43	28	99	253.57	179	267	49.16
Total	141 116	180 505	27.91	46 004	56 187	22.14	15 196	20 221	33.07	12 450	13 242	6.36
Others	19 771	29 112	47.25	3 775	5 368	42.20	1 477	2 235	51.32	1 331	1 466	10.14
Total all industry	160 887	209 617	30.29	49 779	61 555	23.66	16 673	22 456	34.68	13 781	14 708	6.73

Table B.2 (continued)

	Paraná			Santa Catarina			Rio Grande do Sul			Goias		
	1970	1980	1970–80 (%)	1970	1980	1970–80 (%)	1970	1980	1970–80 (%)	1970	1980	1970–80 (%)
Traditional	5416	6232	15.07	3649	4256	16.63	9267	8925	-3.69	2473	3791	53.30
Textiles	151	199	31.79	243	338	39.09	295	343	16.27	9	15	66.67
Clothing, shoes	186	427	129.57	232	545	134.91	1034	2383	130.46	145	243	67.59
Food	3677	3784	2.91	1905	2003	5.14	5092	3593	-29.44	1796	2673	48.83
Beverages	190	107	-43.68	231	153	-23.77	821	471	-42.63	50	43	-14.00
Printing	303	580	91.42	154	235	52.60	467	685	46.68	74	172	132.43
Furniture	823	1066	29.53	812	946	16.50	1276	1157	-9.33	339	611	80.24
Leather	86	69	-19.77	72	36	-50.00	282	293	3.90	60	34	-43.33
Dynamic A	2057	3502	70.25	1605	2498	55.64	3780	5210	37.83	1109	2576	132.28
Nonmetals	1428	2144	50.14	1003	1596	59.12	2308	2973	28.81	950	2192	130.74
Metallurgy	373	922	147.18	261	629	141.00	989	1717	73.61	109	320	193.58
Paper	85	131	54.12	97	111	14.43	80	94	17.50	5	10	100.00
Rubber	67	104	55.22	42	57	35.71	119	138	15.97	27	24	-11.11
Chemicals	98	189	92.86	192	99	-48.44	239	240	0.42	15	26	73.33
Pharmaceuticals	6	12	100.00	10	6	-40.00	45	48	6.67	3	4	33.33
Dynamic B	706	1300	84.14	486	937	92.80	1535	1635	6.51	210	205	-2.38
Machinery	280	669	138.93	218	499	128.90	832	915	9.98	121	77	-36.36
Electrical	107	138	28.97	81	114	40.74	243	183	-24.69	37	25	-32.43
Transport	283	398	40.64	169	247	46.15	373	360	-3.49	46	87	89.13
Plastics	36	95	163.89	18	77	327.78	87	177	103.45	6	16	166.67
Total	8179	11034	34.91	5740	7691	33.99	14582	15770	8.15	3792	6572	73.31
Others	2475	2822	14.02	3041	3484	14.57	3129	3417	9.20	517	1332	157.64
Total all industry	10654	13856	30.05	8781	11175	27.26	17711	19187	8.33	4309	7904	83.43

Table B.3. Total wages ($Cr), by sector, Brazil and selected states (source: IBGE, 1970; 1980).

	Brazil			São Paulo			Minas Gerais			Rio-Guanabara		
	1970	1980	1970–80 (%)	1970	1980	1970–80 (%)	1970	1980	1970–80 (%)	1970	1980	1970–80 (%)
Traditional	4300956	8788890	104.35	2216757	3663928	65.28	258993	527034	126.66	730277	944466	29.33
Textiles	1317037	1996657	51.60	824625	1084025	31.46	91569	136058	48.59	163160	172543	5.75
Clothing, shoes	495823	1793386	261.70	265892	747177	181.01	14217	93282	556.13	82295	178083	116.40
Food	1147251	2539025	121.31	482704	832203	72.40	89189	206710	131.77	156509	255663	63.35
Beverages	277508	360626	29.95	104503	107185	2.57	12486	26004	108.27	71308	56570	−20.67
Printing	631796	1107352	75.27	326278	524049	60.61	28740	69765	142.75	183722	198237	7.90
Furniture	343253	791789	130.67	185620	316634	70.58	16813	45273	169.27	57887	60551	4.60
Leather	88288	200054	126.59	27135	52655	94.05	5979	9941	66.26	15396	22819	48.22
Dynamic A	3822365	9316359	143.73	2305826	5035032	118.36	265597	901221	239.32	557209	881837	58.26
Nonmetals	743362	1941163	161.13	386536	767968	98.68	67987	225977	232.38	105319	159383	51.33
Metallurgy	1443698	4062759	181.41	899723	2414651	168.38	161252	538184	233.75	199912	356079	78.12
Paper	350734	768773	119.19	228112	472047	106.94	8333	23338	180.07	46082	68826	49.36
Rubber	183851	438788	138.67	149539	327978	119.33	3142	12699	304.16	11184	16432	46.92
Chemicals	860797	1818375	111.24	478562	882896	84.49	22068	94042	326.15	194712	205919	5.76
Pharmaceuticals	239923	286501	19.41	163354	169490	3.76	2815	6981	147.98	*	75197	*
Dynamic B	3346835	10946114	227.06	2468972	7180624	190.83	120731	717993	494.70	399571	1072526	168.42
Machinery	1238929	5701265	360.18	815038	3662295	349.34	92942	455288	389.86	113659	499179	339.19
Electrical	734958	1937517	163.62	557441	1368484	145.49	14212	63417	346.22	114564	161798	41.23
Transport	1174427	2604202	121.74	954388	1701655	78.30	12269	183039	1391.88	142733	342270	139.80
Plastics	198521	703129	254.18	142105	448191	215.39	1308	16250	1142.32	28615	69279	142.11
Total	11470156	29051363	153.28	6991555	15879584	127.13	645321	2206248	241.88	1687057	2898828	71.83
Others	829774	3867438	366.08	353882	1468534	314.98	25944	158275	510.07	268156	239162	−10.81
Total all industry	12299930	32918801	167.63	7345437	17348118	136.18	671265	2364523	252.25	1955213	3137990	60.49

Table B.3 (continued)

	Paraná			Santa Catarina			Rio Grande do Sul			Goias		
	1970	1980	1970–80 (%)	1970	1980	1970–80 (%)	1970	1980	1970–80 (%)	1970	1980	1970–80 (%)
Traditional	117250	277561	136.73	134935	463913	243.80	358793	907538	152.94	22878	61493	168.79
Textiles	17099	33083	93.48	73086	189215	158.89	32516	68646	111.11	1524	3722	144.24
Clothing, shoes	3097	20111	549.37	4825	97474	1920.20	96359	335195	247.86	1449	4737	226.95
Food	45852	118020	157.39	32419	98332	203.32	121498	255663	110.43	14726	34395	133.57
Beverages	10384	14091	35.70	4166	7459	79.04	28688	43992	53.35	1263	5360	324.35
Printing	15464	27276	76.38	3981	14182	256.25	28968	51997	79.50	2449	8881	262.65
Furniture	20976	59120	181.84	14575	53678	268.29	25428	81500	220.51	1257	3829	204.58
Leather	4378	5861	33.87	1883	3572	89.70	25336	70543	178.43	210	568	170.69
Dynamic A	91073	262632	189.47	66159	238783	260.92	194231	530480	173.12	8495	57358	575.20
Nonmetals	30469	88894	191.75	20780	97274	368.11	30168	88306	192.71	5121	38126	644.51
Metallurgy	14625	48112	228.97	18556	76966	314.78	97500	241736	147.93	1625	12206	651.11
Paper	26562	43005	61.91	20138	37520	86.31	13260	45306	241.68	285	752	164.02
Rubber	2820	5826	106.61	857	3343	290.10	9331	29294	213.95	776	1141	47.04
Chemicals	16597	76268	359.53	5828	22529	286.56	40613	115761	185.03	406	3088	660.54
Pharmaceuticals	*	1526	*	*	1150	*	3359	10076	199.97	282	2045	625.17
Dynamic B	27963	225566	706.66	34281	209133	510.06	120774	569504	371.55	2043	18509	805.99
Machinery	14249	128858	804.33	14249	124880	776.41	61267	324758	430.07	1079	9395	770.73
Electrical	2677	33238	1141.62	3091	27694	795.96	19984	74103	270.81	394	4659	1082.61
Transport	7827	47777	510.41	6277	26327	319.42	34354	141463	311.78	570	3628	536.55
Plastics	3210	15692	388.85	10664	30232	183.50	5169	29180	464.52	*	826	*
Total	236286	766759	224.50	235375	911829	287.39	673798	2007522	197.94	33416	137361	311.06
Others	104332	219721	110.60	93655	216174	130.82	76041	198714	161.32	2322	19481	738.99
Total all industry	340618	986480	189.61	329030	1128003	242.83	749839	2206236	194.23	35738	156842	338.87

* Data not available.

Table B.4. Total output (SCr), by sector, Brazil and selected states (source: IBGE, 1970; 1980).

	Brazil			São Paulo			Minas Gerais			Rio-Guanabara		
	1970	1980	1970–80 (%)	1970	1980	1970–80 (%)	1970	1980	1970–80 (%)	1970	1980	1970–80 (%)
Traditional	46279051	120201547	159.73	22955679	52922218	130.54	3321403	9665098	190.99	5923630	13224900	123.26
Textiles	10823995	26816063	147.75	6705401	13924549	107.66	650874	2068015	217.73	1128450	2067423	83.21
Clothing, shoes	3933949	16095542	309.14	2306973	7493493	224.82	115359	743513	544.52	578121	1718721	197.29
Food	23542676	57975762	146.26	10087737	23191978	129.90	2188781	5792903	164.66	2537915	6399410	152.15
Beverages	2195112	4398020	100.36	948880	1518165	60.00	75754	303660	300.85	411697	535545	30.08
Printing	2936666	6731476	129.22	1565674	3368791	115.17	114822	290967	153.41	853325	1898748	122.51
Furniture	2078768	6149932	195.85	1113359	2853299	156.28	122306	344172	181.40	314886	431228	36.95
Leather	767885	2034751	164.98	227655	571944	151.23	53507	121869	127.76	99236	173824	75.16
Dynamic A	39395998	177458044	350.45	21063576	90090506	327.71	4359386	19419788	345.47	6838665	22770134	232.96
Nonmetals	4853764	17537164	261.31	2415738	6904568	185.82	586009	2847319	385.88	661702	1746325	163.91
Metallurgy	14528696	57341637	294.68	7148245	29547061	313.35	3117214	11682293	274.77	2827171	8510650	201.03
Paper	2845516	11231090	294.69	1871812	6313107	237.27	80351	530921	560.75	363040	874551	140.90
Rubber	1978049	6252322	216.09	1629861	4891050	200.09	27871	120874	333.69	104349	263403	152.42
Chemicals	12691813	80505119	534.31	6344320	39444980	521.74	531315	4168563	684.57	2882403	10082578	249.80
Pharmaceuticals	2498160	4590714	83.76	1653600	2989739	80.80	16626	69817	319.93	*	1292628	*
Dynamic B	23595712	94592609	300.89	18248516	65690806	259.98	486307	4883483	904.20	2858439	8549758	199.11
Machinery	6636133	31705502	377.77	4611685	21641535	369.28	292210	2043698	599.39	951531	2443191	156.76
Electrical	5483135	21679413	295.38	4300411	14420381	235.33	99588	695927	598.71	605458	1493417	146.66
Transport	9551432	32749152	242.87	8050878	24508118	204.42	83764	1996673	2283.69	933484	3603765	286.06
Plastics	1925012	8458542	339.40	1285542	5120772	298.34	10745	147286	1270.74	367966	1009385	174.31
Total	109270761	392252200	258.97	62267771	208703531	235.17	8167096	33968369	315.92	15620734	44544792	185.16
Others	7244782	25518995	252.24	3104328	11082528	257.00	234859	1118349	376.18	1794798	−251745	−114.03
Total all industry	116515543	417771195	258.55	65372099	219786058	236.21	8401955	35086717	317.60	17415532	44293047	154.33

Table B.4 (continued)

	Paraná			Santa Catarina			Rio Grande do Sul			Goias		
	1970	1980	1970–80 (%)	1970	1980	1970–80 (%)	1970	1980	1970–80 (%)	1970	1980	1970–80 (%)
Traditional	2240290	6740028	200.86	1279475	7683481	500.52	4196643	12689109	202.36	667855	1970749	195.09
Textiles	467951	977649	108.92	454509	2344294	415.79	244361	691995	183.19	36367	93939	158.31
Clothing, shoes	24316	189885	680.91	37163	1493895	3919.84	571304	2821615	393.89	16682	52034	211.92
Food	1428407	4590980	221.41	646931	3168018	389.70	2469801	6399410	159.11	582265	1662629	185.55
Beverages	75718	162232	114.26	28810	82265	185.54	344392	816571	137.10	9702	66116	581.47
Printing	78074	155527	99.20	16238	72610	347.16	129934	296378	128.10	10548	49733	371.49
Furniture	135317	573558	323.86	75972	470335	519.09	164799	871183	428.63	9401	30820	227.84
Leather	30507	90197	195.66	19852	52065	162.26	272052	791957	191.11	2890	15478	435.57
Dynamic A	948230	9940516	948.32	480954	3722725	674.03	2140045	11039492	415.85	63987	701186	995.83
Nonmetals	182346	1053031	477.49	106700	882826	727.39	187011	665928	256.09	28885	482704	1571.12
Metallurgy	112808	594514	427.01	143899	1001821	596.20	690509	2597180	276.13	18258	105236	476.38
Paper	198864	1007777	406.77	167380	818010	388.71	94859	502988	430.25	2445	14934	510.80
Rubber	28323	91160	221.86	7206	25787	257.86	62384	422924	577.94	5271	13426	154.72
Chemicals	425889	7179782	1585.83	55769	973376	1645.37	1080994	6758620	525.22	7565	63670	741.64
Pharmaceuticals	*	14252	*	*	20905	*	24288	91852	278.18	1563	21216	1257.39
Dynamic B	214142	1856753	767.07	407574	2760599	577.32	936580	4420578	371.99	10911	117638	978.16
Machinery	105660	774421	632.94	163235	1174428	619.47	389449	2249361	477.58	5096	31921	526.38
Electrical	15918	443017	2683.12	40677	391837	863.29	245946	659627	168.20	2885	40468	1302.70
Transport	55774	368769	561.18	65641	358281	445.82	259563	1118044	330.74	2930	31528	976.06
Plastics	36790	270546	635.38	138021	836053	505.74	41622	393546	845.52	*	13721	*
Total	3402662	18537297	444.79	2168003	14166806	553.45	7273268	28149179	287.08	742753	2789573	275.57
Others	860404	2682577	211.78	667648	2110567	216.12	614134	1949982	217.52	22029	117584	433.77
Total all industry	4263066	21219873	397.76	2835651	16277373	474.03	7887402	30099161	281.61	764782	2907157	280.13

* Data not available.

Table B.5. Total value added (SCr), by sector, Brazil and selected states (source: IBGE, 1970; 1980).

	Brazil			São Paulo			Minas Gerais			Rio-Guanabara		
	1970	1980	1970–80 (%)	1970	1980	1970–80 (%)	1970	1980	1970–80 (%)	1970	1980	1970–80 (%)
Traditional	18590684	46755287	151.50	9485542	20660787	117.81	1210299	3282078	171.18	2737921	5553624	102.84
Textiles	4976927	10943386	119.88	3068664	5877522	91.53	324428	885910	173.07	581731	848182	45.80
Clothing, shoes	1782971	8277804	364.27	1010138	3507521	247.23	45653	374370	720.03	273528	998605	265.08
Food	7178391	17175573	139.27	3155253	6777962	114.82	633268	1493369	135.82	814240	1894723	132.70
Beverages	1234514	2067970	67.51	514756	687117	33.48	46405	134416	189.66	261352	256705	-1.78
Printing	1958090	4440296	126.77	1028122	2221947	116.12	76433	192284	151.57	579354	1266794	118.66
Furniture	1116058	3054326	173.67	612791	1369405	123.47	61366	154242	151.35	168287	218070	29.58
Leather	343733	795932	131.56	95818	219313	128.88	22746	47488	108.77	59429	70544	18.70
Dynamic A	18829922	64886997	244.60	10654650	34431721	223.16	1766061	6755134	282.50	2934270	7205033	145.55
Nonmetals	3134408	9944183	217.26	1563519	3961804	153.39	370959	1549524	317.71	421680	959388	127.52
Metallurgy	6158995	19686474	219.64	3247598	10638913	227.59	1153946	3620024	213.71	1078565	2421834	124.54
Paper	1364271	5176722	279.45	889758	2763390	210.57	35258	316475	797.60	171659	422880	146.35
Rubber	1038598	2167751	108.72	871525	1623937	86.33	11822	56948	381.71	62605	114022	82.13
Chemicals	5330978	25104821	370.92	2885607	13614176	371.80	182311	1170183	541.86	1199761	2494677	107.93
Pharmaceuticals	1802672	2807047	55.72	1196643	1829600	52.89	11765	41980	256.82	*	792234	*
Dynamic B	11866719	45306510	281.79	8958168	29871439	233.45	308882	2565446	730.56	1542174	4781657	210.06
Machinery	3756203	17346066	361.80	2572281	11516865	347.73	204880	1220472	495.70	540115	1523739	182.11
Electrical	2868636	10866561	278.81	2263888	7019243	210.05	44698	355679	695.74	343092	910316	165.33
Transport	4242403	12929603	204.77	3439412	8854545	157.44	54176	877178	1519.13	503994	1793416	255.84
Plastics	999477	4164282	316.65	682587	2480785	263.44	5128	112116	2086.36	154973	554185	257.60
Total	49287325	156948795	218.44	29098360	84963946	191.99	3285242	12602658	283.61	7214365	17540314	143.13
Others	3990296	17831385	346.87	1862470	6395078	243.37	151474	575478	279.92	1125107	582699	-48.21
Total all industry	53277621	174780180	228.06	30960830	91359024	195.08	3436716	13178136	283.45	8339472	18123013	117.32

Table B.5 (continued)

	Paraná			Santa Catarina			Rio Grande do Sul			Goias		
	1970	1980	1970–80 (%)	1970	1980	1970–80 (%)	1970	1980	1970–80 (%)	1970	1980	1970–80 (%)
Traditional	722466	2111788	192.30	555680	2942945	429.61	1602779	5191664	223.92	165792	530677	220.09
Textiles	140471	328460	133.83	256015	812311	217.29	126883	357400	181.68	16828	35164	108.96
Clothing, shoes	8585	89737	945.28	16822	874718	5099.84	301101	1575874	423.37	5749	21707	277.57
Food	393128	1210923	208.02	207759	886968	326.92	718139	1894723	163.84	124648	389583	212.55
Beverages	49510	75262	52.01	15630	42382	171.16	165970	405253	144.17	5430	29804	448.87
Printing	52184	97122	86.11	10706	47533	343.98	90919	190920	109.99	6914	33872	389.91
Furniture	64670	280336	333.49	40872	260665	537.76	85746	443944	417.74	4766	16821	252.94
Leather	13918	29948	115.17	7876	18362	133.22	114021	323550	183.76	1457	3726	155.73
Dynamic A	400861	3138194	683.04	272201	1636099	501.06	964023	3802638	294.46	32632	372063	1040.18
Nonmetals	119370	578844	384.92	70122	564004	704.32	119454	416935	249.03	18532	278372	1402.11
Metallurgy	53882	240657	346.64	69051	452971	556.00	359925	1175985	226.73	6390	54648	755.21
Paper	86330	449445	420.61	100328	284574	183.64	51314	277476	440.74	1059	5066	378.37
Rubber	12947	35838	176.80	3292	14043	326.58	36922	156934	325.04	2309	7026	204.29
Chemicals	128332	1822970	1320.15	29408	307393	945.27	379724	1717496	352.30	3545	16577	367.62
Pharmaceuticals	*	11161	*	*	13112	*	16684	57813	246.52	797	10375	1201.72
Dynamic B	112953	864095	665.00	190824	1314142	588.67	491706	2398696	387.83	6861	68822	903.09
Machinery	54546	335030	514.22	54546	568009	941.34	228319	1250606	447.74	3493	21124	504.77
Electrical	8935	266543	2883.13	17266	156778	808.02	109072	369506	238.77	1736	23387	1247.15
Transport	29287	157595	438.10	34991	178689	410.67	133096	573294	330.74	1632	17070	945.96
Plastics	20185	104928	419.83	84021	410666	388.77	21219	205290	867.48	*	7241	*
Total	1236280	6114797	394.61	1018705	5893186	478.50	3058508	11392998	272.50	205285	971562	373.27
Others	402713	1316089	226.81	350126	1177695	236.36	314394	1045196	232.45	11699	69154	491.11
Total all industry	1638993	7430887	353.38	1368831	7070881	416.56	3372902	12438194	268.77	216984	1040716	379.63

* Data not available.

Table B.6. Average plant size (number of workers), by sector, Brazil and selected states (source: IBGE, 1970; 1980).

	Brazil			São Paulo			Minas Gerais			Rio-Guanabara		
	1970	1980	1970–80 (%)	1970	1980	1970–80 (%)	1970	1980	1970–80 (%)	1970	1980	1970–80 (%)
Traditional	13.54	19.49	43.95	19.23	25.99	35.16	9.29	14.03	51.06	21.70	24.10	11.05
Textiles	64.58	62.29	−3.54	57.00	58.39	2.44	110.34	74.45	−32.53	129.29	103.72	−19.78
Clothing, shoes	19.10	29.98	56.97	19.24	29.01	50.79	9.72	20.19	107.78	25.67	31.15	21.38
Food	7.95	12.60	58.41	10.52	16.96	61.24	5.55	9.84	77.19	11.47	15.34	33.76
Beverages	12.22	20.00	63.73	18.76	29.86	59.13	5.05	7.58	50.10	39.51	52.13	31.95
Printing	17.57	17.06	−2.90	19.06	19.78	3.75	11.80	10.76	−8.82	24.86	22.19	−10.75
Furniture	8.02	13.79	71.88	12.26	21.69	76.86	5.45	9.70	77.90	14.39	14.95	3.87
Leather	12.99	25.83	98.90	18.59	33.24	78.81	8.78	13.08	48.96	55.56	97.05	74.67
Dynamic A	18.29	20.64	12.80	28.92	36.32	25.59	15.08	16.81	11.51	29.64	35.43	19.54
Nonmetals	9.32	10.13	8.67	14.60	17.43	19.39	7.57	8.39	10.83	26.14	24.03	−8.10
Metallurgy	27.57	36.91	33.86	33.93	48.08	41.68	34.96	45.86	31.16	26.75	34.97	30.71
Paper	56.87	63.05	10.86	62.21	65.94	6.01	37.22	48.11	29.27	54.56	59.94	9.87
Rubber	33.74	44.36	31.49	59.70	73.51	23.13	9.72	17.46	79.58	30.48	38.07	24.90
Chemicals	39.46	47.74	20.99	53.77	51.74	−3.77	21.71	40.90	88.44	55.56	49.80	−10.35
Pharmaceuticals	59.01	69.12	17.14	90.31	85.72	−5.08	14.28	27.28	91.10	*	86.07	*
Dynamic B	34.19	59.93	75.26	48.39	67.94	40.41	21.72	59.65	174.69	41.09	70.53	71.66
Machinery	26.75	55.21	106.34	34.47	58.77	70.49	27.21	64.84	138.27	36.31	71.81	97.76
Electrical	36.60	72.97	99.35	52.69	78.22	48.45	12.85	40.86	217.98	34.36	53.29	55.07
Transport	47.71	70.62	48.03	85.05	114.87	35.07	18.43	70.63	283.33	68.05	100.18	47.22
Plastics	32.47	44.83	38.08	33.25	43.71	31.48	14.64	31.87	117.64	33.63	48.27	43.54
Total	17.02	24.32	42.83	26.52	37.33	40.73	11.66	17.96	54.05	26.17	33.06	26.32
Total all industry	16.38	23.46	43.28	25.90	37.01	42.93	11.18	17.30	54.75	25.91	32.39	25.02

Table B.6 (continued)

	Paraná			Santa Catarina			Rio Grande do Sul			Goias		
	1970	1980	1970–80 (%)	1970	1980	1970–80 (%)	1970	1980	1970–80 (%)	1970	1980	1970–80 (%)
Traditional	6.99	12.37	76.89	12.84	26.29	104.73	12.29	26.15	112.81	4.61	6.56	42.19
Textiles	28.81	36.12	25.34	90.25	103.41	14.58	32.82	44.24	34.77	92.56	79.33	−14.29
Clothing, shoes	7.84	17.84	127.47	11.78	53.12	350.91	32.88	38.53	17.19	6.14	9.94	61.73
Food	4.76	8.99	89.03	6.67	13.64	104.57	7.84	20.32	159.32	4.08	5.85	43.26
Beverages	12.12	25.49	110.35	5.06	11.14	120.08	7.95	15.78	98.45	8.30	20.60	148.25
Printing	12.52	11.05	−11.79	8.32	13.31	59.94	14.00	13.80	−1.42	9.91	11.83	19.39
Furniture	8.84	16.01	81.03	7.78	15.75	102.47	7.38	18.39	149.25	3.06	4.04	32.05
Leather	13.86	29.64	113.83	10.13	26.33	160.08	27.74	52.05	87.67	2.90	7.50	158.62
Dynamic A	13.03	16.09	23.43	13.96	22.33	59.98	13.77	18.81	36.57	4.09	6.89	68.53
Nonmetals	8.74	11.90	36.18	9.82	17.46	77.71	6.02	8.95	48.68	3.57	5.71	60.10
Metallurgy	11.72	12.87	9.86	20.09	26.24	30.64	24.03	25.86	7.58	5.90	10.99	86.36
Paper	61.44	62.69	2.37	51.43	61.03	18.65	52.35	85.57	63.47	19.20	24.20	26.04
Rubber	10.16	15.66	54.10	7.02	13.68	94.83	21.41	37.04	72.97	10.00	14.83	48.33
Chemicals	41.46	46.63	12.47	10.54	36.12	242.65	29.07	51.50	77.18	5.20	22.92	340.83
Pharmaceuticals	*	23.67	*	*	47.33	*	16.09	31.17	93.72	18.00	125.50	597.22
Dynamic B	11.36	27.77	144.43	23.26	39.02	67.77	18.26	50.86	178.59	4.28	18.17	324.46
Machinery	12.56	26.47	110.68	26.85	40.90	52.33	17.03	47.62	179.69	3.83	19.77	416.57
Electrical	8.06	40.65	404.62	11.69	45.34	287.83	20.29	67.54	232.82	5.11	31.84	523.32
Transport	8.95	21.78	143.33	12.23	19.66	60.71	20.58	58.30	183.32	5.37	13.21	145.96
Plastics	30.78	43.31	40.70	135.39	79.62	−41.19	14.37	35.22	145.13	*	16.13	*
Total	8.89	15.36	72.84	14.04	26.56	89.20	13.30	26.29	97.63	4.44	7.05	58.76
Total all industry	10.51	16.73	59.23	12.90	23.88	85.11	12.28	23.78	93.63	4.32	6.75	56.27

* Data not available.

Table B.7. Average wage ($Cr) by sector, Brazil and selected states (source: IBGE, 1970; 1980).

	Brazil			São Paulo			Minas Gerais			Rio-Guanabara		
	1970	1980	1970–80 (%)	1970	1980	1970–80 (%)	1970	1980	1970–80 (%)	1970	1980	1970–80 (%)
Traditional	3.68	4.68	27.07	4.49	5.08	13.00	2.77	3.88	39.89	4.32	4.90	13.25
Textiles	3.84	5.29	37.65	4.45	5.81	30.62	2.82	3.90	38.05	3.82	5.06	32.23
Clothing, shoes	3.01	3.90	29.39	3.38	3.82	12.88	2.03	3.11	53.22	3.27	3.62	10.73
Food	3.08	4.08	32.49	4.13	4.65	12.62	2.72	3.71	36.25	3.39	4.41	29.91
Beverages	4.73	6.16	30.19	5.43	6.24	14.90	2.73	4.42	61.79	6.71	7.48	11.54
Printing	6.51	7.79	19.77	7.83	8.12	3.66	4.42	7.61	72.17	7.35	7.95	8.09
Furniture	3.26	4.53	39.08	4.21	4.74	12.57	2.18	3.48	59.26	3.60	4.04	12.37
Leather	3.35	4.74	41.59	3.60	4.44	23.11	2.54	3.96	55.80	4.86	5.73	17.97
Dynamic A	5.18	7.00	35.30	6.02	7.89	31.05	4.19	6.54	55.98	6.18	7.01	13.41
Nonmetals	3.14	4.44	41.20	4.03	5.41	34.18	3.15	4.35	38.14	3.87	4.92	27.30
Metallurgy	5.41	7.64	41.27	6.04	8.03	33.00	4.74	7.83	65.00	5.79	7.11	22.75
Paper	5.24	7.16	36.68	5.93	8.03	35.25	3.24	5.45	67.96	5.21	5.32	1.95
Rubber	5.59	7.77	38.88	6.29	8.68	37.92	3.48	4.95	42.39	4.64	5.20	11.96
Chemicals	8.25	11.14	35.07	8.33	10.99	31.97	6.09	10.45	71.66	11.38	11.30	−0.72
Pharmaceuticals	7.79	8.42	8.15	8.74	8.91	1.92	4.20	5.56	32.59	*	8.40	*
Dynamic B	6.74	9.26	37.50	7.18	9.74	35.59	5.90	9.69	64.20	5.98	9.00	50.54
Machinery	6.87	10.59	54.29	7.42	11.30	52.18	6.61	1.057	60.08	4.24	9.95	134.48
Electrical	6.36	7.96	25.03	6.49	8.29	27.75	4.61	7.76	68.40	7.86	8.68	10.33
Transport	7.42	9.26	24.83	8.08	9.85	21.91	4.24	9.29	119.01	7.33	9.13	24.56
Plastics	4.66	5.92	26.85	4.75	5.96	25.30	3.19	5.15	61.44	4.75	5.38	13.08
Total	4.77	6.62	38.64	5.73	7.57	32.14	3.64	6.08	66.78	5.18	6.62	27.89
Total all industry	4.67	6.69	43.37	5.70	7.61	33.63	3.60	6.09	69.00	5.48	6.59	20.28

Table B.7 (continued)

	Paraná			Santa Catarina			Rio Grande do Sul			Goias		
	1970	1980	1970–80 (%)	1970	1980	1970–80 (%)	1970	1980	1970–80 (%)	1970	1980	1970–80 (%)
Traditional	3.10	3.60	16.30	2.88	4.15	43.98	3.15	3.89	23.41	2.01	2.47	23.31
Textiles	3.93	4.60	17.13	3.33	5.41	62.44	3.36	4.52	34.73	1.83	3.13	70.97
Clothing, shoes	2.12	2.64	24.35	1.77	3.37	90.72	2.83	3.65	28.80	1.63	1.96	20.62
Food	2.62	3.47	32.32	2.55	3.60	41.02	3.04	3.50	15.00	2.01	2.20	9.54
Beverages	4.51	5.17	14.55	3.56	4.38	22.83	4.39	5.92	34.70	3.04	6.05	98.77
Printing	4.07	4.26	4.46	3.11	4.53	45.96	4.43	5.50	24.13	3.34	4.37	30.69
Furniture	2.88	3.46	20.80	2.31	3.60	56.13	2.70	3.83	41.82	1.21	1.55	27.98
Leather	3.67	2.87	−21.97	2.58	3.77	45.88	3.24	4.63	42.79	1.21	2.23	84.70
Dynamic A	3.40	4.68	37.76	2.95	4.28	44.96	3.73	5.41	45.09	1.87	3.23	72.48
Nonmetals	2.44	3.49	42.70	2.11	3.49	65.54	2.17	3.32	52.84	1.51	3.04	101.54
Metallurgy	3.35	4.05	21.14	3.54	4.66	31.74	4.10	5.44	32.75	2.53	3.47	37.28
Paper	5.09	5.22	2.62	4.04	5.54	37.22	3.17	5.63	77.89	2.97	3.11	4.73
Rubber	4.14	3.58	−13.63	2.91	4.29	47.54	3.66	5.73	56.51	2.87	3.21	11.52
Chemicals	4.08	8.65	111.85	2.88	6.30	118.79	5.85	9.37	60.20	5.21	5.18	−0.47
Pharmaceuticals	*	5.37	*	*	4.05	*	4.64	6.74	45.17	5.22	4.07	−21.99
Dynamic B	3.49	6.25	79.23	3.03	5.72	88.60	4.31	6.85	58.91	2.27	4.97	118.65
Machinery	4.05	7.28	79.65	2.43	6.12	151.34	4.32	7.45	72.33	2.33	6.17	164.88
Electrical	3.11	5.92	90.78	3.26	5.36	64.15	4.05	6.00	47.95	2.08	5.85	180.79
Transport	3.09	5.51	78.38	3.04	5.42	78.56	4.48	6.74	50.59	2.31	3.16	36.84
Plastics	2.90	3.81	31.66	4.38	4.93	12.69	4.14	4.68	13.19	*	3.20	*
Total	3.25	4.52	39.17	2.92	4.46	52.82	3.47	4.84	39.40	1.98	2.97	49.40
Total all industry	3.04	4.25	39.86	2.90	4.23	45.53	3.45	4.83	40.27	1.92	2.94	53.11

* Data not available.

Table B.8. Value added per worker ($Cr), by sector, Brazil and selected states (source: IBGE, 1970; 1980).

	Brazil			São Paulo			Minas Gerais			Rio-Guanabara		
	1970	1980	1970–80 (%)	1970	1980	1970–80 (%)	1970	1980	1970–80 (%)	1970	1980	1970–80 (%)
Traditional	15.93	24.91	56.39	19.23	28.64	48.92	12.97	21.70	67.36	16.21	28.80	77.63
Textiles	14.52	28.98	99.64	16.56	31.51	90.31	10.00	25.37	153.70	13.63	24.86	82.31
Clothing, shoes	10.84	18.00	66.09	12.85	17.92	39.49	6.52	12.48	91.49	10.85	20.27	86.82
Food	19.28	27.61	43.24	27.01	37.91	40.33	19.33	26.80	38.63	17.65	32.67	85.06
Beverages	21.06	35.54	67.82	26.76	40.02	49.53	10.15	22.83	125.02	24.59	33.96	38.10
Printing	20.17	31.25	54.96	24.68	34.43	39.48	11.76	20.98	78.43	23.19	50.79	119.05
Furniture	10.60	17.48	65.00	13.90	20.49	47.48	7.97	11.85	48.65	10.46	14.56	39.20
Leather	13.02	18.84	44.69	12.73	18.48	45.22	9.67	18.91	95.64	18.77	17.73	-5.52
Dynamic A	25.50	48.78	91.29	27.80	53.93	93.95	27.88	49.01	75.83	32.56	57.30	75.96
Nonmetals	13.25	22.73	71.54	16.30	27.90	71.13	17.17	29.81	73.61	15.48	29.62	91.38
Metallurgy	23.07	37.02	60.46	21.81	35.40	62.35	33.96	52.66	55.09	31.25	48.36	54.75
Paper	20.36	48.19	136.62	23.14	46.98	102.98	13.73	73.91	438.31	19.42	32.66	68.16
Rubber	31.60	38.38	21.45	36.68	42.98	17.17	13.08	22.19	69.71	26.00	36.08	38.79
Chemicals	51.08	153.80	201.11	50.20	169.43	237.49	50.29	130.03	158.56	70.12	136.86	95.19
Pharmaceuticals	58.53	82.54	41.03	64.01	96.14	50.19	17.53	33.45	90.78	*	88.51	*
Dynamic B	23.89	38.34	60.51	26.06	40.52	55.46	15.10	34.63	129.33	23.07	40.11	73.89
Machinery	20.82	32.23	54.83	23.43	35.52	51.63	14.56	28.35	94.67	20.16	30.36	50.62
Electrical	24.84	44.63	79.66	26.36	42.53	61.35	14.49	43.52	200.30	23.55	48.91	107.28
Transport	26.79	45.97	71.56	29.12	51.25	76.03	18.73	44.51	137.69	25.89	47.86	84.84
Plastics	23.48	35.04	49.22	22.84	32.98	44.39	12.51	35.54	184.12	25.74	43.00	67.02
Total	20.52	35.76	74.30	23.85	40.51	69.88	18.55	34.70	87.13	22.14	40.07	80.95
Total all industry	20.22	35.54	75.74	24.02	40.10	66.95	18.44	33.93	83.97	23.36	38.04	62.87

Table B.8 (continued)

	Paraná			Santa Catarina			Rio Grande do Sul			Goias		
	1970	1980	1970-80 (%)	1970	1980	1970-80 (%)	1970	1980	1970-80 (%)	1970	1980	1970-80 (%)
Traditional	19.08	27.40	43.60	11.86	26.30	121.79	14.07	22.24	58.04	14.54	21.34	46.85
Textiles	32.28	45.70	41.58	11.67	23.24	99.08	13.10	23.55	79.76	20.20	29.55	46.27
Clothing, shoes	5.88	11.78	100.31	6.16	30.22	390.90	8.86	17.16	93.79	6.45	8.99	39.30
Food	22.48	35.59	58.32	16.36	32.46	98.48	17.99	25.95	44.19	17.02	24.95	46.58
Beverages	21.51	27.60	28.31	13.37	24.87	86.02	25.42	54.53	114.47	13.08	33.64	157.09
Printing	13.75	15.16	10.22	8.35	15.19	81.91	13.91	20.19	45.22	9.43	16.65	76.55
Furniture	8.89	16.43	84.78	6.47	17.49	170.37	9.11	20.86	129.09	4.60	6.82	48.30
Leather	11.68	14.64	25.38	10.80	19.38	79.34	14.58	21.21	45.53	8.37	14.61	74.50
Dynamic A	14.95	55.71	272.67	12.15	29.33	141.40	18.51	38.80	109.55	7.20	20.98	191.26
Nonmetals	9.57	22.70	137.16	7.12	20.24	184.44	8.60	15.67	82.24	5.47	22.23	306.63
Metallurgy	12.33	20.27	64.43	13.17	27.44	108.36	15.14	26.49	74.93	9.94	15.53	56.31
Paper	16.53	54.55	230.01	20.11	42.01	108.90	12.25	34.49	181.53	11.03	20.93	89.77
Rubber	19.01	22.00	15.73	11.16	18.00	61.33	14.49	30.71	111.90	8.55	9.74	130.78
Chemicals	31.59	206.85	554.80	14.53	85.96	491.62	54.66	138.96	154.22	45.45	27.81	-38.80
Pharmaceuticals	*	39.30	*	*	46.17	*	23.04	38.64	67.70	14.76	20.67	40.03
Dynamic B	14.08	23.94	70.00	16.88	35.94	112.91	17.55	28.85	64.40	7.63	18.48	142.09
Machinery	15.50	18.92	22.06	9.32	27.83	198.64	16.12	28.70	78.08	7.54	13.88	83.97
Electrical	10.37	47.51	358.17	18.23	30.33	66.36	22.12	29.90	35.16	9.19	29.38	219.86
Transport	11.56	18.18	57.28	16.93	36.81	117.42	17.34	27.32	57.52	6.61	14.86	124.85
Plastics	18.22	25.51	39.98	34.48	66.98	94.28	16.98	32.93	93.99	*	28.07	*
Total	17.01	36.07	112.07	12.64	28.85	128.20	15.77	27.48	74.29	12.19	20.97	72.01
Total all industry	14.64	32.05	118.90	12.08	26.50	119.27	15.50	27.26	75.80	11.66	19.52	67.33

* Data not available.

References

Addis C, 1988, "The Brazilian motor vehicle complex: a successful and ongoing struggle to improve quality and capabilities despite the very difficult political moment", working paper, International Motor Vehicle Program, Massachusetts Institute of Technology, Cambridge MA

Alonso W, 1980, "Five bell shapes in development" *Papers of the Regional Science Association* **45** 5 – 16

Alonso W, Medrich E, 1978, "Spontaneous growth centers in twentieth century American urbanization", in *Systems of Cities* Eds L Bourne J Simmons (Oxford University Press, New York) pp 349 – 361

Amin S, 1974 *Accumulation on a World Scale: Critique of Theories of Underdevelopment* (Monthly Review Press, New York)

Angel D, 1988, "Production, labor markets and location: a case study of the US semiconductor industry", unpublished PhD dissertation, Department of Geography, University of California, Los Angeles, CA

Arthur, W B, 1983, "On competing technologies and historical small events: the dynamics of choice under increasing returns", Department of Economics, Stanford University, Stanford, CA

Azzoni C R, 1986, "Indústria e reversão de polarizaçao no Brasil", Série Ensaios Econômicos number 58, Instituto de Pesquisas Econômicas, São Paulo

Bacha E L, 1978, "Emprego e distribuição da renda", in *Os Mitos de uma Década (Ensaios da Economía Brasileira)* E L Bacha (Paz e Terra, Rio de Janeiro) pp 57 – 136

Bacha E L, Taylor L, 1980, "Brazilian income distribution in the 1960s: 'facts', model results and the controversy", in *Models of Growth and Distribution for Brazil* Eds L Taylor, E L Bacha, E Cardoso, F J Lysy (Oxford University Press, New York) pp 296 – 342

Bagnasco A, 1977 *Tre Italie: La Problematica dello Svillupo* (Il Mulino, Bologna)

Becattini G, 1987 *Mercato e Forze Locali: Il Distretto Industriale* (Il Mulino, Bologna)

Becker D, Sklar R (Eds), 1987 Post-imperialism: International Capitalism and Development in the Late Twentieth Century (Rienner, Boulder, CO)

Bellandi M, 1986, "Capácita innovativa diffusa e distretti industriali", working paper, Department of Economics, University of Florence, Florence

Bianchi P, Giordani M G, Pasquini F, 1988, "Industrial policy in Italy at a regional level", paper presented to the Regional Science Association, European Congress, Stockholm; copy available from NOMISMA, Strada Maggiore 44, 40125 Bologna)

Boudeville J R, 1966 *Problems of Regional Economic Planning* (Edinburgh University Press, Edinburgh)

Brenner R, 1977, "The origins of capitalist development: a critique of neo-Smithian Marxism" *New Left Review* number 104, 25 – 92

Cano W, 1981 *Raízes da Concentração Industrial em São Paulo* (Queiroz, São Paulo)

Cano W, 1985 *Desequilibríos Regionais e Concentração Industrial no Brasil, 1930 – 1970* (Global, São Paulo)

Cardoso F H, 1977, "The consumption of dependency theory in the United States" *Latin American Research Review* **12** 7 – 24

CEDEPLAR, 1986, Relatório da Pesquisa (Report on Research Project) Centro de Desenvolvimento e Planejamento Regional, Universidade Federal de Minas Gerais, Belo Horizonte

Coase R H, 1937, "The nature of the firm" *Economica* **4** 386 – 405

Conjuntura Ecónomica Instituto Brasiliero de Geografía e Estatística, Rio de Janeiro

Corbridge S, 1988, "Marxism and development studies: beyond the impasse", unpublished manuscript, Department of Geography, Syracuse University, Syracuse, NY

Cusumano M, 1985 *The Japanese Automobile Industry* (Harvard University Press, Cambridge, MA)

de Bresson C, 1986, "Spatial patterns in the propagation of innovation", WP 1986–89, Department of Economics, Concordia University, Montreal

de Janvry A, 1981 *The Agrarian Question and Reformism in Latin America* (Johns Hopkins University Press, Baltimore, MD)

de Oliveira F, 1977 *Elogía para Uma Re(li)gião: SUDENE, Planejamento e Conflítos de Classe* (Paz e Terra, Rio de Janeiro)

Dillinger W, Hamer A, 1982, "Sources of growth in manufacturing employment in non-metropolitan areas", WP 17, National Spatial Policies in Brazil Project, World Bank, Washington, DC

Diniz C C, Lemos M B, 1986, "Mudança no padrão regional Brasileiro: determinantes e implicações" *Análise Conjuntura Curitíba* **8**(2) 32–42

El Shaks S, 1972, "Development, primacy, and systems of cities" *Journal of Developing Areas* **7** 11–36

Emmanuel A, 1972 *Unequal Exchange: A Study of the Imperialism of Trade* (Monthly Review Press, New York)

Evans P, 1979 *Dependent Development: The Alliance of Multinational, State, and Local Capital in Brazil* (Princeton University Press, Princeton, NJ)

Evans P, 1987, "Class, state, and dependence in East Asia: lessons for Latin Americanists", in *The Political Economy of the New Asian Industrialism* Ed. F Deyo (Cornell University Press, Ithaca, NY) pp 203–226

Fei G, Ranis G, 1964 *Development of the Labor Surplus Economy: Theory and Policy* (Richard D Irwin, Homewood, IL)

Fields G S, 1977, "Who benefits from economic development? A re-examination of Brazilian growth in the 1960s" *American Economic Review* **67** 570–582

Fishlow A, 1965 *American Railroads and the Transformation of the Ante-bellum Economy* (Harvard University Press, Cambridge, MA)

Friedmann J, 1966 *Regional Development Policy: A Case Study of Venezuela* (MIT Press, Cambridge, MA)

Friedmann J, 1973 *Urbanization, Planning and National Development* (Sage, Beverly Hills, CA)

Friedmann J, Douglass M, 1978, "Agropolitan development: towards a new strategy for regional planning in Asia", in *Growth Pole Strategy and Regional Development Policy* Eds F-C Lo, K Salih (Pergamon Press, Oxford) pp 163–192

Fröbel F, Heinrichs J, Kreye O, 1980 *The New International Division of Labor* (Cambridge University Press, Cambridge)

Gambetta D, 1988, "Mafia: the price of distrust", in *Trust* Ed. D Gambetta (Basil Blackwell, Oxford) pp 158–175

Geiger P, Davidovich F, 1986, "The spatial strategies of the state in the political–economic development of Brazil", in *Production, Work, Territory: The Geographical Anatomy of Industrial Capitalism* Eds A J Scott, M Storper (Allen and Unwin, Winchester, MA) pp 281–298

Gershuny J, 1982 *Social Innovation and the Division of Labor* (Oxford University Press, Oxford)

Gordon D M, 1988, "The global economy: new edifice or crumbling foundations?" *New Left Review* number 172, 24–64

Gore C, 1984 *Regions in Question* (Methuen, New York)

Habbakuk H J, 1962 *American and British Technology in the Nineteenth Century: The Search for Labour-saving Inventions* Cambridge University Press, Cambridge)

Hamer A M, 1982, "Brazilian industrialization and economic concentration in São Paulo: a survey", National Spatial Policies in Brazil Project, World Bank, Washington, DC)

Hansen N, 1978 *Human Settlement Systems: International Perspectives on Structure, Change and Public Policy* (Ballinger, Cambridge, MA)

Hareven T, 1978 *Amoskeag: Life and Work in an American Factory City* (Pantheon Books, New York)

Harrod R, 1973 *Economic Dynamics* (St Martin's Press, New York)

Hecht S, 1986, "Report to World Resources Institute on Amazonian Development Policies", World Resources Institute, Washington, DC)

Hecht S, Cockburn A, 1989 *The Fate of the Forest: Developers, Destroyers and Defenders of the Amazon* (Verso, London)

Henderson J V, 1982, "Urban economies of scale in Brazil", WP 24, National Spatial Policies in Brazil Project, World Bank, Washington, DC)

Hirschman A O, 1958 *The Strategy of Economic Development* (Yale University Press, New Haven, CT)

Hirschman A, 1965 *Política Económica de America Látina* (Fundo de Cultura, Rio de Janeiro)

Holanda S de B, 1936 *Raízes do Brasil* (Olympio, Rio de Janeiro)

Holmes J, 1986, "The organization and locational structure of production sub-contracting", in *Production, Work, Territory: The Geographical Anatomy of Industrial Capitalism* Eds A J Scott, M Storper (Allen and Unwin, Winchester, MA) pp 80–105

Homem de Melo F, 1986, "Estabilidade de preços alimentos e intervenções: uma nova postura governamental" *Revista de Economía Política* 6(3) 25–34

Hoselitz B, 1953, "The role of cities in the economic growth of underdeveloped countries" *Journal of Political Economy* 61 195–208

Hoselitz B, 1955, "Generative and parasitic cities" *Economic Development and Cultural Change* 2 278–294

Humphrey J, 1982 *Fazendo o Milagre* (Ed. Vozes, Petropolis, Brazil)

IBGE, 1970 *Censo Industrial* Instituto Brasileiro de Geografia e Estatistica, Rio de Janeiro

IBGE, 1980 *Censo Industrial* Instituto Brasileiro de Geografia e Estatistica, Rio de Janeiro

Jayet H, 1983, "Chômer plus souvent en région urbaine, plus longtemps en région rurale" *Économie et Statistique* 153 7–57

Kaldor N, 1970, "The case for regional policies" *Scottish Journal of Political Economy* 17 337–347

Kaldor N, 1972, "The irrelevance of equilibrium economics" *The Economic Journal* 8 1237–1255

Kalecki M, 1971 *Selected Essays on the Dynamics of the Capitalist Economy, 1922–1970* (Cambridge University Press, Cambridge)

Kipnis B, 1983, "Clusters and complexes of medium-sized urban manufacturing systems: two case studies in Brazil" *Professional Geographer* 35(1) 32–39

Kuznets S, 1955, "Economic growth and income inequality" *American Economic Review* 45 1–28

Kuznets S, 1966 *Modern Economic Growth: Rate, Structure, and Spread* (Yale University Press, New Haven, CT)

Lampard E, 1986, "The New York metropolis in transformation: history and prospect", in *The Future of the Metropolis* Eds H J Ewers, J B Goddard, A Matzerath (de Gruyter, New York) pp 27–110

Langenbruch J, 1981, "O encabecimento das armaduras urbanas nacionais: uma revisão" *Geografia* 11(12) 1–104

Lewis W A, 1954, "Economic development with unlimited supplies of labor" *Manchester Bulletin of Economic and Social Studies* 22 139–191

Lipietz A, 1977 *Le Capital et son Espace* (La Découverte, Paris)

Lipietz A, 1986, "New tendencies in the international division of labor: regions of accumulation and modes of regulation", in *Production, Work, Territory: The Geographical Anatomy of Industrial Capitalism* Eds A J Scott, M Storper (Allen and Unwin, Winchester, MA) pp 16 – 39

Lipton M, 1977 *Why Poor People Stay Poor: A Study of Urban Bias in World Development* (Smith, London)

Lo F-C, Salih K, 1981, "Growth poles, agropolitan development, and polarization reversal: the debate and search for alternatives", in *Development from Above or Below?* Eds W Stöhr, D R F Taylor (John Wiley, New York) pp 123 – 152

Macedo R, 1980, "Distribuição funcional na indústria da transformação: aspectos da parcela salarial" *Estudos para o Planejamento 23* (IPEA, Brasilia)

Markusen A, 1985 *Profit Cycles, Oligopoly, and Regional Development* (MIT Press, Cambridge, MA)

Martinelli F, 1986 *"Producer Services in a Dependent Economy* unpublished doctoral dissertation, Department of City and Regional Planning, University of California at Berkeley, Berkeley, CA)

Mera K, 1973, "On the urban agglomeration and economic efficiency" *Economic Development and Cultural Change* 21 316 – 340

Morley S, Smith G W, 1977, "The choice of technology: multinational firms in Brazil" *Economic Development and Cultural Change* 25 239 – 264

Myrdal G, 1957 *Rich Lands and Poor* (Harper, New York)

Nelson S, Winter S, 1982 *An Evolutionary Theory of Economic Change* (Harvard University Press, Cambridge, MA)

Nichols V, 1969, "Growth poles: an evaluation of the propulsive effects" *Environment and Planning* 1 193 – 208

Noyelle T, Stanback T, 1983 *Services/The New Economy* (Rowman and Littlefield, Totowa, NJ)

Ohno T, 1982, "How the Toyota production system was created" *Japan Economic Studies* 10(4) 83 – 103

Parr J, 1973, "Growth poles, regional development, and central place theory" *Papers and Proceedings of the Regional Science Association* 31 172 – 212

Perroux F, 1955, "Note sur la notion de 'Pôle de croissance'" *Économie Appliquée* January – June, pp 307 – 320

Piore M, Sabel C, 1984 *The Second Industrial Divide* (Basic Books, New York)

Portes A, Benton L, 1984, "Industrial development and labor absorption: a reinterpretation" *Population and Development Review* 10 589 – 611

Portes A, Walton J, 1981 *Capital, Labor, and the International System* Academic Press, New York)

Pratten C F, 1971 *Economies of scale in manufacturing industry* (Cambridge University Press, Cambridge)

Pred A, 1966 *The Spatial Dynamics of US Urban – Industrial Growth, 1860 – 1914* (Harvard University Press, Cambridge, MA)

Pred A, 1977 *Systems of Cities in Advanced Economies* (Hutchinson, London)

Richardson H, 1973 *Regional Growth Theory* (Macmillan, London)

Richardson H, 1980, "Polarization reversal in developing countries" *Papers of the Regional Science Association* 45 67 – 85

Robinson J, 1956 *The Accumulation of Capital* (Macmillan, London)

Rondinelli D, 1977 *Secondary Cities in Developing Countries* (Sage, Beverly Hills, CA)

Rosenberg N, 1972 *Technology and American Economic Growth* (Harper Torch Books, New York)

Rostow W W, 1961 *The Stages of Economic Growth* (Cambridge University Press, Cambridge)

Russo M, 1985, "Technical change and the industrial district: the role of interfirm relations in the growth and transformation of ceramic tile production in Italy" *Research Policy* **14** 329-343

Sabel C, 1982 *Work and Politics: the Division of Labor in Industry* (Cambridge University Press, Cambridge)

Schmitz H, 1988, "Flexible specialization—a new paradigm of small-scale industrialization?", working paper, Institute of Development Studies, University of Sussex, Brighton, Sussex

Schumpeter J, 1934 *The Theory of Economic Development* (Harvard University Press, Cambridge, MA)

Schumpeter J, 1942 *Capitalism, Socialism, and Democracy* (Harper and Row, New York)

Scott A J, 1988a *Metropolis: From the Division of Labor to Urban Form* (University of California Press, Berkeley, CA)

Scott A J, 1988b *New Industrial Spaces* (Pion, London)

Scott A J, Storper M, 1987, "High technology industry and regional development: a theoretical critique and reconstruction" *International Social Science Journal* **112** 215-232

Sen A K, 1963, "Neo-classical and neo-Keynesian theories of distribution" *Economic Record* **39** 53-66

Senhor 1986, "A Califórnia é aqui", issue number 292 A, pp 100-110

Sforzi F, 1988, "The geography of industrial districts in Italy", manuscript, Department of Economics, University of Florence, Florence

Singer P, 1977 *Desenvolvimento Econômico e Evolução Urbana* (Ed. Nacional, São Paulo)

Sirmans C F, 1977, "City size and unemployment: some new estimates" *Urban Studies* **14** 91-101

Sraffa P, 1926, "The laws of returns under competition" *Economic Journal* **36** 535-551

Stanbach T, Noyelle T, 1983 *Cities in Transition* (Allanheld, Osmun, Totowa, NJ)

Stiglitz J, 1974, "Alternate theories of wage determination and unemployment in LDCS: the labor turnover model" *Quarterly Journal of Economics* **87** 194-227

Stöhr W, Taylor D R F (Eds), 1979 *Development from Above or Below? A Radical Reappraisal of Spatial Planning in Developing Countries* (John Wiley, New York)

Stöhr W, Todtling F, 1979, "Spatial equity: some antitheses to current regional development doctrine", in *Spatial Inequalities and Regional Development* Eds H Folmer, J Oosterhaven (Martinus Nijhoff, Boston, MA) pp 130-160

Storper M, 1984, "Who benefits from industrial decentralization? Social power in the labor market, income distribution, and spatial policy in Brazil" *Regional Studies* **18** 143-164

Storper M, 1989, "The transition to flexible specialization in industry" *Cambridge Journal of Economics* **13** 273-305

Storper M, Christopherson S, 1987, "Flexible specialization and regional industrial agglomerations" *Annals of the Association of American Geographers* **77** 104-117

Storper M, Scott A J, 1989a, "The geographical foundations and social regulation of flexible production complexes", in *The Power of Geography* Eds J Wolch, M Dear (Unwin Hyman, London) pp 21-40

Storper M, Scott A J, 1989b, "Work organization and local labor markets in an era of flexible production", WP 30, Studies in Labor Flexibility, International Labour Office, Geneva

Storper M, Walker R, 1989 *The Capitalist Imperative: Territory, Technology, and Industrial Growth* (Basil Blackwell, Oxford)

Sunkel O, 1985 *America Latína y la Crisis Economica Internacional: Ocho Tésis y una Propuesta* (Grupo Editor Latinoamericana, Buenos Aires)

Sutcliffe R B, 1971 *Industry and Underdevelopment* (Addison-Wesley, Reading, MA)

Townroe P, Keen D, 1984, "Polarization reversal in the state of São Paulo, Brazil" *Regional Studies* **18** 45 – 54

Townroe P, Roseman P, 1982, "Sectoral influences on spatial change in manufacturing: São Paulo State, Brazil, 1960 – 1975", WP 10 (revised), National Spatial Policies in Brazil Project, World Bank, Washington, DC

Verdoorn P, 1980, "Verdoorn's law in retrospect: a comment *Economic Journal* **90** 382 – 385

Vieira da Cunha P, 1983, "Protected wages, the urban informal sector, and market segmentation: a theoretical comment", Instituto de Planejamento Econômico e Social, Rio de Janeiro

Vieira da Cunha P, Bonelli R, 1978, "Estrutúra de salários industriais no Brasil: um estudo sôbre a distribuição de salários médios em 1970" *Pesquisa e Planejamento Econômico* **8** 117 – 168

Vipond J, 1974, "City size and unemployment" *Urban Studies* **11** 39 – 46

Walker R A, 1985, "Is there a service economy?" *Science and Society* **49**(1) 42 – 83

Walker R, Storper M, 1981, "Capital and industrial location" *Progress in Human Geography* **5** 473 – 509

Wheaton W, Shishido H, 1981, "Urban concentration, agglomeration economies and the level of economic development" *Economic Development and Cultural Change* **30**(1) 17 – 30

World Bank 1984 *World Development Report* (The World Bank, Washington, DC)

Young A, 1928, "Increasing returns and economic progress" *Economic Journal* **38** 527 – 542

Zipf G, 1949 *Human Behavior and the Principle of Least Effort* (Hafner Press, New York)

Author index

Subject index

n indicates footnote

Agglomeration 92
  and division of labor 16, 19
  and economic growth 11 – 32, 92
  and external economies 14, 31 – 32, 88
  and infrastructure 21
  and interfirm transactions 14
  and labor migration 72 – 77
  and localization 20
  and productivity 21, 45
  and urbanization 19, 25
  diseconomies of 6, 9, 31 – 32, 101
  economies of 11, 14, 27, 45, 91, 115
Agriculture (see also rural)
  and wages 92 – 94
  regions 93
Aircraft industry 14, 108
Appropriate technology 79, 85 – 87
Artisanal production 13, 88
Authoritarianism 75, 80
Automobile industry 11, 14, 108

Banking industry 19
Big Push strategies (see also industrialization) 84, 88 – 89
Branch plants (see also industry location) 27, 96
Brazil 59, 83

Capital, accumulation of 11 – 32, 66 – 71, 88 – 89, 108
Central place theory 5
Ceramic tile industry 111
City (see also rank size rule, urbanization, agglomeration)
  hierarchy, see urban hierarchy
  primate 5, 8n4
  size 4
  systems 5, 9
Class relations, Brazil 81
Comparative advantage 22, 117
Consumption
  and income distribution 66 – 71, 80, 99 – 101
  durable goods 67, 86, 106
  luxury goods 99
Contracts (see also subcontracting, linkages, production system) 13, 15
Core – periphery relations (see also uneven development, region, rural) 9, 89 – 92
Coronéis 82

Demand, elasticity of (see also consumption, income distribution, wages) 73
Demographic transition (see also population) 3
Depolarization, see polarization reversal
Deskilling (see also labor, skills) 110
Diminishing returns (see also neoclassical economics, scale) 21
Disintegration (see also production system, linkages, division of labor, agglomeration) 12, 87
  horizontal 12, 22
  vertical 12, 13, 19, 22, 85
Division of labor (see also production system) 9, 11, 23, 74, 84 – 89
  and agglomeration 16, 28
  and equilibrium 20 – 23
  and growth 22
  and telecommunications 19
  roundaboutness of 22
  social 11, 12, 13, 28
  technical 11, 28, 110

Economies of scale, see scale, economies of
Electronics industry (see also microelectronics) 11, 28, 32, 108
Endogenous development 105 – 118
Estado Nôvo 37, 38
External economies (see also scale, transactions, agglomeration, division of labor) 4, 18, 31 – 32, 87n22, 88, 96

Factor
  demand 67 – 71
  markets, regional 9
  prices 23, 86
    spatial 22, 29 – 32
    wages 31
  supplies 67
Flexible production 107 – 118
  and agglomeration 115
  regulation of 116
  specialization 89
Fordism (see also mass production) 105 – 118

Place index